THE
NO EXCUSES
GUIDE TO
SOUL
MATES

STACEY DEMARCO & JADE-SKY

THE
NO EXCUSES
GUIDE TO
SOUL
MATES

YOU CAN ATTRACT A GREAT RELATIONSHIP
& STOP MAKING MISTAKES IN LOVE

ROCKPOOL
PUBLISHING

A Rockpool book
Published by Rockpool Publishing
24 Constitution Road, Dulwich Hill, NSW 2203, Australia
www.rockpoolpublishing.com.au

First published in 2009
Copyright © Stacey Demarco and Jade-Sky, 2009

National Library of Australia Cataloguing-in-Publication entry

Demarco, Stacey, 1965-

The no excuses guide to soul mates : you can attract a great relationship and
stop making mistakes in love / Stacey Demarco and Jade-Sky.

9781921295218 (pbk.)

Interpersonal attraction.
Mate selection.
Soul mates.
Jade-Sky.

646.77

Edited by Gabiann Marin
Cover and internal design by Corey Bell, The Factory Creative
Typeset in Garamond 12 pt
Printed and bound by I-Book Printing Ltd in China
10 9 8 7 6 5 4 3 2 1

CONTENTS

ACKNOWLEDGEMENTS

STACEY:

Writing a book with someone else can be, in some ways, harder than writing it yourself. You need to not just think about what you have to express but listen, learn and co-operate with someone equally as passionate as you, but who may see things in a different way than you do.

This weaving of ideas, this melding of techniques, this meeting of the minds is really where it's at. It is really where things get exciting, challenging and so totally magical. It is what I believe is the strength of this book.

So Jade-Sky, my co-author and Companion Soul Mate, thank you for the co-creation. Thank you for adding a deliciously different set of ingredients to this particular pie.

To Richard Martin, who made the path clearer, my deep gratitude. Strawberry blondes really do have more fun.

Thank you to my husband, Adam Rehak, my Romantic Soul Mate. You who I asked and cast for, but who came into my life better, brighter and 'more' than I ever imagined. Goddess, I owe you one for him!

Special thanks to Lisa Hanrahan at Rockpool for her enthusiasm and insight.

A salute to all those brave people who allowed us to take their stories and utilise them here. You are trailblazers and teachers and I thank you!

And finally, as always, my deep gratitude to The Goddess who loves and guides me and who creatively facilitates everywhere and every day.

JADE-SKY:

A big thank you to all of the people below:

To my co author Stacey, I couldn't think of anyone else I would rather be working and writing with. You are my true friend, kindred spirit and Companion Soul Mate – thank you for your creativity, passion and true spiritual gifts. I am looking forward to the journey we share together and I am sure our wolves will always keep us on track.

To my husband Adam, it was evident when we were just 12 and 14 years old at sailing club that you were my Romantic Soul Mate. Thank you for the ups, the downs and the in betweens and most importantly for being you, I love you! To my three beautiful children Lachlan, Zane and Lillijana, I love you and appreciate you. I thank the Universe every day for each of you being gifted into my life!

To all of my family and friends who have put up with me and my winding path, my different way of life and my crazy schedule, I appreciate you all and love you. You know who you are!

To Richard, my manager, friend, confidant and Companion Soul Mate, thank you for believing in me and for pushing me to higher ground. You are truly a gift!

To Lisa Hanrahan and the team at Rockpool Publishing, thank you for having faith in this book and for all of your support and professionalism.

To each and every special client who allowed us to share their stories.

And last but not the least, to my Spirit Guides and passed loved ones, you are a constant source of support, knowledge and love. Thank you for all that you do.

INTRODUCTION

MYTHS & MONSTERS OF THE HEART

When we were children, most of us had a boogie man or monster who lived in the closet or under the bed. Eventually, we grew out of this terror, naturally and normally, by finding out more about the world and living our life a little more fearlessly. Our mythical boogie man just went away.

However, it seems that for some of us, the monsters have again risen. There seems to be a more frightening boogie man than that of our childhood, one that we just haven't grown out of.

The name of that boogieman?

The Soul Mate.

For some of us it is now the myths and monsters of the heart who stalk us, making us sweat in the night, leaving us sleepless with an enormous fear of that empty side of our bed.

It is our belief that never before has there been more intense collective fear of being alone and being partner-less. Instead of feeling connected and partner-free there is a wave of desperation and misunderstanding, causing all manner of complex game playing, pain and co-dependence.

But how can we slay this new mythological monster? How can we expose this dreaded relationship boogieman?

By shining an honest light upon it.

Both Jade and I enjoy successful spiritual consultancies and we work with literally thousands of people every year who want something better for themselves. Sometimes our clients are quite 'spiritually' or religiously aligned and therefore have developed strong beliefs around certain subjects. We often speak together about our work (within strict confidentiality of course) and often one of us would bring up a recurring belief that would surface from a number of people repeatedly.

The conversations would often go something like this:

> *Jade: Do you ever get someone thinking that they can't do something because they have had a past life that restricts them now?*
>
> *Stacey: Yes, I have clients like that. Actually, lots of them! ... Oh, and another thing that people often think is that they have met the one soul mate for them, it didn't work and now they will be ...*
>
> *Jade: Alone forever?*
>
> *Stacey: Yes! How did you know?*
>
> *Jade: So many people think that. And what about the idea that there is only one person for them ...*
>
> *Stacey: Oh, THE ONE. As in: my life won't be complete unless I meet THE ONE?*
>
> *Jade: You got it. It's all so ... so limiting!*

After a number of these frustrating conversations we decided that instead of just discussing it and wondering why, we should be doing something about it.

Wouldn't it be good for everyone to get clear, real and grounded about all this stuff? Wouldn't it be beneficial to take a group and tell them about what the real deal is? Offer them some spiritual and non spiritual perspectives? Expose them to what the consensus is saying about this topic? Demonstrate that whilst it is useful to have a spiritual perspective on things, there is a problem if some of their 'spiritual beliefs' don't help them, if in fact, they hinder them!

This is where the concept for this book, and our 'Soul Mates' workshops came from. The goal here is to provide guidance that is presented in a simple and honest way, enabling people to move forward … with no excuses.

Within this book, we are dedicated to giving you a no-holds-barred, no B.S. approach, without all of the airy fairy, new age jargon.

While we both do come from spiritual perspectives (Stacey from the witchcraft tradition and Jade from a psychic medium paradigm) this doesn't mean we are not grounded, rational and anchored in the modern world. We do not feel the need to push our particular beliefs on to you in this book and will give you plenty of room to decide which side of the fence you wish to sit. Facts are facts, beliefs are beliefs and there is a difference.

For all intents and purposes, everything that is written in this book has come from our research and personal experiences, interacting with thousands of our clients in our own personal practices and the documentation of results. You'll find lots of case studies showing how things work, and these are always the experiences of 'normal' everyday people such as yourself.

It's very definitely a 'What Works' approach.

Our methods can look a little 'tough love', after all we are asking for courage and action, and that can be more uncomfortable than fairy dust. They do not leave much room for excuses, but they are compassionate and effective. And isn't that really what you are after … results?

Throughout the book there will be times where we have to refer to a source that some people may like to call God, Allah, Goddess, Spirit,

Higher Power … there are too many terms to list here but for ease of reference and to keep this book as apolitical or non-denominational as we can, we will use the term *the Universe*, which we believe can encompass all religious beliefs and spiritual concepts.

Additionally, this is a book written by two people. When we refer to 'we' it is both of us: Stacey and Jade. If one of us has a differing opinion we will certainly own this by referring to who believes what.

There is no coincidence that you picked this book up or that you are already sitting somewhere reading this book. We hope that it gives you not only the answers you seek, but gets you thinking about changing things in a practical way and encourages you forward, towards your ideal partnership, with more confidence.

As for the term 'Soul Mate', you either love it or hate it. (The term even invokes division between us!). You may not be in a relationship currently or you may be, but we are imagining either way, you would like to be living within a great soulful relationship. This book will certainly facilitate this, whether or not you use the term Soul Mate. For those of you who are slightly wary of the term, that's fine, and we ask that you be patient with us, because by the end of the book you may feel a little less emotionally charged about it, even if you never use it!

Thank you for entrusting us with your valuable time, heart and brain space. We believe that together we will be shining the light on your relationship monsters and banishing them for good. We look forward to working with you.

With love
Stacey Demarco & Jade-Sky

SECTION 1

IS THERE SUCH A THING AS
A SOUL MATE?

We understand that for a lot of people, even hearing the term Soul Mate makes them at the very least sceptical, at worst nauseous. Stacey herself used to feel that way.

Stacey heartily disliked the idea that there was this one person for her and that she was incomplete without them. She also didn't much like the idea that somehow she was fated to meet this person and if she messed it up, well that would be that and she would never be happy. And then of course there was the awful consequence if she didn't meet them – she would be alone forever or have to settle for someone that wasn't her Soul Mate.

Wow. Seemed like the odds were pretty well stacked against her!

But Stacey has always had faith that things were designed a little better than that.

So, she thought, perhaps she may have had the wrong idea about Soul Mates and years ago she decided to do some substantial research about where the idea came from and what the alternatives were. This way, she could … and you can … make your mind up about the whole concept.

We think it's important that we share this information with you so that you know it isn't just the 'spiritual' that gets us all fired up. In fact much of the physical feelings of attraction are indeed out of our conscious control and therefore we don't think much about them. However if we understand the tricks our own body and brain play upon us, we can deduct what is left, if anything, for the idea of a spiritual concept such as Soul Mates.

BIOLOGY OR SPIRITUALITY?

So, your eyes meet across that crowded room.

You see nothing in the room besides those eyes. That mouth.

You are aware your heart is beating hard.

You sweat a little.

They smile at you. You lower your eyes and smile back.

You blush.

You feel like they are the only one in the room.

You feel desired, watched.

You feel so very, very, very good.

Euphoric. Excited.

Maybe you will go over for a chat. In fact, your legs are doing that all by themselves.

That face, those eyes, that mouth.

That mouth is saying 'Hello' and nothing else matters.

Ah! This scene has been playing in a party near you for a long time; perhaps it was even playing in a cave somewhere a really long time ago. That incredible feeling of 'love at first sight' or at least 'love by end of the night'.

Could it be that this intense connection is actually a sure sign you've found The One?

Well, scientists would beg to differ.

They would just say you've just fallen hook, line and sinker into the Biology of Love.

Let's get specific:

When we sight someone we find attractive the body kicks into overdrive.

The neurotransmitters, dopamine and noradenaline, get released into the body from nerve cells, and turn on other nerve cells. Dopamine is involved in memory, pleasure, problem solving, motivation and some circulatory function. Large doses of dopamine make us feel good; very good.

Noradrenaline is primarily responsible for maintaining blood pressure but is implicated in everything you could imagine in the central nervous system – emotional pathways included. It also assists us to focus sharply. Large doses of noradrenaline make us feel intensely aware.

Then a substance called PEA (phenylethylamine) is released into the mix, which stimulates the body to speed up and release *even more* dopamine and noradrenaline. Hey, now we're cookin'!

So let's imagine that larger than usual amounts of these substances are running rampant around your body. The results are blushing, a huge energy boost, feeling nervous, anticipation, heart palpitations, and a general increase in awareness and vitality.

And then, the endorphins kick in.

Endorphins are the pain killer and pleasure-delivering chemicals in our bodies. Remember when you are exercising and it gets harder and you are just about to give up and then suddenly you feel much more energetic and you get a second wind? That's endorphins. We are sure at some stage you have been laughing and dancing for hours on end at a club, lost in the fun and music, only to feel the painful consequences of exercising for hours the next day after the natural drop in endorphins occurs!

Endorphin functions also involve stopping anything that inhibits dopamine and noradrenaline, so now we have a veritable tsunami of love, happy and natural party drugs in our system.

Yet this is just the beginning! This is only pre-sex!

When we actually do get together for sex, our body is not only flooded with endorphins but a chemical called oxytocin. Oxytocin is one of the most frequently studied body substances and is one of the key enablers of orgasm and bonding in both men and women. It is really the 'trust' pill.

A recent study also showed that those of us with naturally high levels of oxytocin are able to form relationships with all manner of people more easily, but, on the flip side of the coin, can get taken in by lies and cons more often. People with higher levels of oxytocin can also end up with distrust issues as they sometimes are unable to balance who they really can trust, so it's easier to trust no-one. By the way, women have naturally higher levels and this is thought to be because of the role oxytocin plays in ensuring attachment between mother and baby.

One of the key ways that oxytocin is triggered in women is indeed through breast stimulation. Now since the whole modern dating process is now speeded up and men often get to stimulate women's breasts (foreplay) earlier in the courting process, this can often skew a woman's view of the seriousness of a relationship.

If the female body is flooded with oxytocin, the body tricks us into believing that more bonding is occurring than actually is. Is it any wonder that women often view foreplay and sex as more of an indicator of a serious love interest than that of a man? Is it no wonder that men are able to more easily mate and then leave, seemingly emotionally unaffected?

But back to our party scenario …

Our eyes lock and the body starts to get to work. All of these natural chemicals are being injected into the blood at a much higher than usual rate. As a result our heart pumps harder; we feel the buzz of adrenalin. We are able to focus more intently on the object of our desire, and block almost everything else out. That headache we felt a minute before is gone, gone, gone. We feel more aware, more alive, sexier, as the blood is pumping at a harder and faster rate than before, particularly to our extremities – and that includes our genitalia. At the same time, all that adrenalin and noradrenaline is whizzing its way through our neural pathways and we feel edgy, anxious but, strangely, happier and more confident. We now feel courageous enough to take the chance of walking right on over to start a conversation.

Then, if that 'why don't you come up for coffee' ends in 'hey why don't you stay till breakfast,' we are injected with another set of bonding hormones that do their darnedest to keep us together, enjoying each other sexually as long as possible and as painlessly as possible.

And why?

For the very same reason as all the other animals on the planet … to breed!

The fact is that our bodies (and our brains for that matter) have evolved to bring us together long enough to mate (like just about every other organism on earth, so don't feel too special), and keep us together long enough to look after young.

There is so much of this chemical cocktail racing around your body that if a doctor was to inject you with these levels, firstly it would be illegal and secondly, you would be advised not to operate heavy machinery! In fact, anyone in the throes of a relationship under 12 months duration should actually wear L plates on their car. L for Love!

The body can keep this powerful induction up for around two years, which, by the way, is the average time for a couple to make the decision to either commit to each other or split up. Even though it's agony – it's ecstasy at the same time, and we want to do it again and again. It's a pretty powerful and addictive combination.

We have more news for you. On top of the body playing tricks on you, your culture is also casting a relationship trance powerful enough to keep you captive.

ROMANTIC LOVE AND WHY IT CAN SUCK …

The popular idea of romantic love is essentially a new one. Certainly we can see evidence of traditions of infatuation in ancient Greek texts and courtly love (a romantic idolisation of 'the other' outside marriage) beginning in the 12th century within the court of Eleanor of France, but it is really not until the 1900's that romantic love, in all its fullness, really hits its straps.

Marriage in between these two periods was generally a way of building alliances and wealth. Women were little more than pawns and property, generally married off in their early teens. Considering that average life expectancy didn't go much beyond 40, this seemed quite a sensible act at the time.

By the 1900s, the idea of a romantic love, that could extended into après-marriage, was a bold one. Prior to this wooing and idolisation of another pre-marriage was common, however the idea that one should feel this intensity for longer periods and during the marriage was unusual.

By the 1920s, in the Western Democracies, the idea of dating as a way to find and select a mate had became more popular, coinciding with a more emancipated view of women. As women and men were free to 'try before they buy' (not necessarily always sexually) the active wooing (read romanticised) period became longer or more frequent, with more and more rules and expectations. Society still deemed marriage the norm and therefore the ultimate goal but there was a yearning and strong pressure for there to be a continuation of this intense romantic period after marriage to prove that this was a perfect partnership. Nothing was as important as this new 'coupledom' and the idea of extended families and networks were made increasingly redundant.

This more equal approach had great benefits for the couple, but as we began to look to *only* the other for the diversity of partnership, financial advantages, love and mating, we did a strange thing. We began to project the idea that satisfaction of our major needs of happiness and fulfilment rested with us having a life-long mate who made everything whole and perfect. The idea that there was one person, our other half or sometimes better half, became the prevalent belief behind dating and finding a mate.

On top of all of this, our life expectancy grew longer. Now it was possible that someone could spend 60–70 years married to the same person, a statistical rarity less than 100 years before. Layer over this the influence of the media, in particular the Hollywood (or Bollywood) love story with thousands of happy-ever-after endings, and imagine the unrealistic expectations we were starting to have of real life.

Now we have a situation where we are expected to try before we buy (but not too much), bond, successfully partner, have and keep the pre-partnered romantic intensity constantly for as long as we live (and that can be a loooong time) and look to the 'other' to complete our emotional, social and physical needs.

Is it any wonder that there is such pressure to find and keep this one partner for life?

SOUL MATES: FACT OR FICTION

You may be wondering, especially after all the biological and cultural facts of attraction and commitment you have just read, why we think there are Soul Mates at all. If it's all about cultural expectations and base biology then what proof do we have that Soul Mates even exist?

Simply because the biological and cultural facts just don't explain the different Soul Mate relationships that we have both experienced in our own lives. Nor explain the countless experiences of clients, friends and family members who have gone through their own Soul Mate relationships.

And possibly even more interestingly, the concept that the soul has a number of different 'partners' is an enduring one that crosses many different times, traditions and cultures. The idea of Soul Mates is not new; in ancient Greece, the famous philosopher Plato wrote about Soul Mates in his 'Symposium', theorising that:

' … humans originally consisted of four arms, four legs, and a single head made of two faces, but Zeus feared their power and split them all in half, condemning them to spend their lives searching for the other half to complete them.'

Soul Mate stories can also be traced as far back as 3000BCE Egypt, with the famous story of brother and sister Osiris and Isis, Egyptian Gods as well as Soul Mates, who had a love so strong that death itself could not separate them.

There are too many references to Soul Mates from various time periods and cultures to be listed here, in particular the Hindu tradition has a wide variety of Soul Mate relationships of different kinds, but there is one reference that stands out to us which resonates with the western romantic part of our souls. It is the Celtic term 'anam cara'.

'In the Celtic tradition, there is a beautiful understanding of love and friendship. One of the fascinating ideas here is the idea of soul-love; the old Gaelic term for this is *anam cara*. *Anam* is the Gaelic word for soul and *cara* is the word for friend. So *anam cara* in the Celtic world was the 'soul friend'. In the early Celtic church, a person who acted as a teacher, companion or spiritual guide was called an *anam cara.*'

Anam Cara.

John O'Donohue, author, poet, philosopher, and scholar

So there has been evidence of Soul Mates throughout the ages, but the difference between our Hollywood inspired kind of soul mate and how the ancients viewed the idea are worlds apart. In most ancient references to Soul Mates, there was more than one type.

More than one type you say? What about the idea of 'The One?' Is it possible that there could be more than one type of Soul Mate? That The One could actually be The Many?

THERE IS NOT JUST ONE SOUL MATE

Speaking from our personal experience and viewpoint we believe that there is not just one Soul Mate per person.

When you look at how many millions of people there are in the world, do you really think that the Universe would be so cruel as to only give us one true Soul Mate, only one chance at happiness?

There are many different Soul Mates that come into our lives in various forms. Pets, friends, family members, work colleagues – any of these can be a Soul Mate connection. We believe it is a myth that you must be 100% linked intimately with your one true love, your one Mr or Mrs Right. In fact your Soul Mate does not have to be that one person in your life that makes your life complete.

We believe that there are four basic types of Soul Mate connections that you may come across in your life, whether you are aware of it or not, they are as follows:

- Karmic
- Companion

- Twin
- Romantic

Karmic Soul Mates

Karmic Soul Mates are very common in all of our lives. They are people that come into your life for a specific reason: so that both of you can work out any past or current life issues together.

These very strong relationships can occur with anyone, but most often with people such as a parent, co-worker, boss, or even a lover that has shared at least one previous life with you. The point of these relationships is to work out karma with this other soul.

Have you ever had an intense feeling or an instant recognition around someone that you have only just met? There may be an intense attraction, or the opposite may occur – you may have an instant dislike or aversion to a person for no apparent reason as soon as you meet them. Often the person may feel the same way about you. This is often the indicator of a Karmic Soul Mate connection.

Karmic Soul Mate relationships are frequently difficult or challenging, involving a lot of chaos and strife. This is because each person has a set of karmic lessons which they have brought into their current life. These kinds of relationships have key lessons for both parties to learn.

In the case of a negative Karmic Soul Mate relationship, the energy between the two people can be quite hurtful, both emotionally and physically. It can be incredibly hard to leave a negative Karmic Soul Mate relationship because the attraction is so strong and this can often be seen in abusive relationships.

There is a lot of unfinished business between Karmic Soul Mates, however not all karma is bad or negative karma. There can be good karma as well. A positive Karmic relationship is where one or both people recognise the negative situation and actively work through, and let go of, the challenging issues. In this way a Karmic Soul Mate can help each partner move forward and be happy in another relationship.

Once the Karmic Soul Mates have learnt their lessons, usually they each go their own separate ways to progress further on their spiritual path. Sometimes however, they may not be able to resolve their differences in this life. In fact, the Karmic Soul Mates can sometimes actually create additional karma between them which will have to be sorted out in another life.

Karmic Soul Mates usually are not meant to be long term life partners, they are simply in each other's lives to help each other move through something from the past and then they can move on. Often people think they can try to turn a negative or abusive Karmic relationship into a long term loving, Romantic or Companion Soul Mate relationship … this can be very damaging for everyone concerned. The key with these kinds of relationships is to learn the lesson and move on if you need to.

Some key examples of lessons to be learnt in a Karmic Soul Mate relationship are:

- How to learn to be independent and to stand your ground in relationships
- What to put up with and what to walk away from ethically
- Strength, independence and the ability to feel safe and secure in our own power
- We will attract what we need to learn or fix about ourselves

We have all heard of the usual Karmic relationship stories of a man and woman or family members who have a tumultuous relationship which is quite abusive, yet they continue to stay together in a never-ending cycle of self destruction and pain. However Karmic relationships are not only limited to intimate partnered or married relationships. Any kind of relationship, no matter how long you have known each other, can be a Karmic Soul Mate relationship.

A Karmic Soul Mate relationship can have both positive and negative effects.

With the following case study you will see that a positive experience can certainly come from a 'negative' Karmic Soul Mate relationship.

KARMIC SOUL MATE – NATASHA*

(*Names changed for privacy)

Natasha, a bright spark of a woman, with pixie-like features and a cheeky lust for life, asked during one of her readings if she would ever meet a life partner, a guy that she could be happy with in a relationship.

Information came through for Natasha about the new man that would be coming her way, but Natasha was warned that with this relationship came a double-edged sword: she would need to balance her feelings and emotions very carefully and keep a level head. She was happy with that as she bounced out of the office; she said she would keep her eye out for the new man.

It was almost a year later that Natasha arrived back in the office for another reading. She went on to tell the story of what had happened since her last reading. She had met a guy as predicted. This man was very creative, adventurous and highly strung.

She went on to tell how intense the relationship was. It started out very much a passionate adventure, which was very exciting, and she soon moved in with him. Unhappily though, over a short time, Natasha started to feel like things were changing – and not for the better.

Her man did not let her live her life her own way. He became extremely controlling and started to question everything that Natasha did. Natasha went from being fun, exciting and free to being depressed

THE NO EXCUSES GUIDE TO SOULMATES

and repressed in a controlling relationship. After much anguish and heartache Natasha decided to break free from the relationship

She told the man of her decision, but he didn't want to let Natasha go so easily. He tried everything he could to stop her from leaving him. He was both verbally and physically abusive towards her.

It took a while for Natasha to escape this relationship; she finally plucked up enough courage and physically left the man. She moved back to her old neighbourhood and slowly began to heal herself by finding her passion for life again.

There is a happy ending to this, though; Natasha did learn a great deal about herself and what she wanted in a relationship. She also learnt that she didn't need to have a partner in her life; she could survive and thrive without one, but if someone else did come along that allowed her to be more independent this would be better. She would also be more careful not to jump in head first (living with the man so soon) without testing the waters over time first.

KARMIC SOUL MATE – JULIE*

Julie, a 50 year old artist, also met a Karmic Soul Mate. Julie was recovering from a 20 year marriage that had drained her lust for life. Whilst she had been faithful to her husband, he had not returned that favour and she was feeling less than confident in her womanhood.

Julie met a younger man at work. Twenty years younger. She enjoyed his company but on a platonic level. She couldn't believe it when he asked her out for dinner. She agreed out of shock more than a rational answer and enjoyed herself so much that her first date with him ended up lasting to the following morning!

Julie, though, was quite educated in the different kinds of Soul Mates and saw the relationship for what it was: a lesson for her. She said in an email: I am enjoying this because I feel like a woman again. The sex is great, I am desired by this gorgeous younger man, but I know I will want more eventually. He is not here with me for the long term, but for a term of enjoyment!

After three months the relationship petered out with no regrets on either side. She now is confidently dating a man she believes is more Romantic Soul Mate material.

Companion Soul Mates

We choose our Companion Soul Mates before we are born, to reconnect within our lives for support and spiritual growth; they encourage us and offer a helping hand when we need it.

The Companion Soul Mate relationship is very stable, comfortable, respectful, loving, and full of commitment and friendship. Even though this kind of relationship is stable and loving it is not always smooth sailing, but it can endure the hard times and can often last a lifetime.

Every day we meet Companion Soul Mates; they come into our lives in a variety of different ways. They may be a kind stranger on the bus who smiles and helps you through your day or a teacher who inspires you. Your pet may be your best friend, your Companion Soul Mate that keeps you company when you are feeling lonely, sick or down.

There does not need to be a sexual intimacy between Companion Soul Mates, often the relationship is based solely on friendship and companionship - hence the name. The highly-fuelled emotional highs and lows and intense sexual tension that appears in other types of Soul Mate relationships usually doesn't appear in Companion Soul Mate relationships.

If there is an intimate relationship between the Companion Soul Mates, it is a grounded relationship which is based on love, not drama or pain. That is the difference between Karmic and Companion Soul Mates. A Companion Soul Mate will not start an intimate relationship with their Companion Soul Mate if they are partnered to someone else, without finishing it first. A Karmic Soul Mate, because of the lessons or past hurts, may jump head first into a relationship and may want their cake and eat it too. They may try to have the current intimate relationship without thinking or worrying about the effect it will have on the other people involved.

Some key examples of lessons to be learnt in a Companion Soul Mate relationship are:

- How to let go of past hurts and to trust people again
- To be open and honest with your deepest feelings
- To be able to give and receive love equally without any guilt
- How to have a positive supportive relationship which does not revolve around sex or ego

With the following case study you will see that even though there is a very strong emotional bond between Companion Soul Mates it doesn't automatically mean that they have to take their relationship to the next level. Companion Soul Mates don't have to have an intimate sexual relationship.

COMPANION SOUL MATES – JOSH* AND CASSIE*
(*Names changed for privacy)

Josh and Cassie were the best of friends because they had so much in common, they both had a love for art and good food. Some would say they were very similar to Will and Grace, a very popular American comedy sitcom which highlights the relationship between Will, a single gay man, and his best friend Grace, a straight single woman. The only difference was that Josh was not gay, so this put a lot of pressure on Josh and Cassie's friendship because other people wanted to see them as a romantic couple.

Josh was an attractive, down to earth guy with rugged good looks and clear bright blue eyes. Cassie was tall with blonde hair and a big cheeky grin; she was not lacking in the looks department either.

To everyone else, Josh and Cassie seemed like the perfect pair, they would be ideal romantic relationship partners. They both knew what each other liked and disliked, had similar interests and friends, and both of them wanted to settle down and have kids.

There was just one big problem. Cassie and Josh were Companion Soul Mates, they did not have any fire or chemistry between them. They did not feel drawn to each other physically in a sexually intimate way. Whilst other people would love to see them as a couple, they did not need to try and force their relationship to be intimate, because they knew it was special just the way it was. Besides it would be like kissing their brother or sister, it just wouldn't feel right to them.

It was important to each of them to keep their special friendship but they both wanted an intimate relationship again with a partner of their own.

It was tough going trying to find someone else who would be able to complete them in the way that their friendship did, but they both decided it was time to try and get the ball moving within their relationship areas.

It's important that they didn't try to force themselves to feel something which wasn't there for them sexually. This would be a recipe for disaster, as it often is for other people who 'settle' for a Companion Soul Mate. At time of writing, they are both still looking for their ideal partners and they have each other for support and companionship when they need it.

Twin Soul Mates

In the media or through word-of-mouth, you may have heard of stories that seem too bizarre to be true – women leaving their kids, husbands and normal stable lives behind to run away with someone who they have never even met in person, someone that they have only met on the internet.

There are also stories of prison wardens who fall in love with an inmate and risk everything to have a secret relationship with the prisoner; some have even gone as far as to try to free the inmate or commit crimes for them.

Why do these kinds of things happen? How could someone who is usually quite stable, normal and balanced behave so irrationally? Why would they throw their lives away on a whim on a fantasy or dream of a fairytale romance?

One answer to this is that each of these examples above and various other cases like them are most likely Twin Soul Mates, the pull is so strong, so electric, that it can almost feel like a life or death situation. The physical sensations are so intense that you can feel as if you would physically die if you are not with your Twin Soul Mate.

The Twin Soul Mate relationship is one of the most powerful soul connections you can have with another person. The Twin Soul is the other half or twin of your soul. In saying that it is important to understand that each twin is a complete soul in their own right, they are not half a soul.

Each person has only one Twin Soul, otherwise it would be triplets or quads etc … each twin continues on their own separate path after they split. The separate twin souls each gather their own human experiences before they come back together to share some of their last physical lifetimes together.

When the Twin Souls reunite it is to balance out both the female and male energies. Twin Souls do not need to be of opposite sexes. We have met many Twin Souls who are of the same sex.

Often Twin Souls are drawn back together to be of service to help the greater scheme of things universally and also to help their twin to become closer to spiritual enlightenment. Twin Souls arrive when you are least expecting it and can throw your life into a tail spin.

Even though Twin Souls spend some lives together and some apart, the link is never broken. If your Twin Soul decides not to reincarnate with you in a particular life, he or she may choose to be your spirit guide or helper from the spirit world.

Usually a Twin Soul will recognise the other twin's energy when they meet. It may not be an instant recognition, like in the romantic movies and novels, but there will be an intensity that is hard to explain. Sometimes one twin will feel the connection more strongly than the other, this can be extremely difficult for the twin who has had the soul recognition and wants to share that experience with the twin who hasn't realised the connection yet.

We want you all to know that not all Twin Soul relationships are beautiful, easy and carefree like in the Hollywood type fairytales. They can be extremely painful emotionally and, if you aren't ready, it can be hard to accept the level of intensity and commitment a Twin Soul brings to you.

Sometimes your Twin Soul is sent to you merely to open you up spiritually so you can each advance at a more rapid rate. You may not be able to live together and be with each other in an intimate relationship this life. They can be difficult to live with as they are the other half of you, your mirror, they reflect everything you like and don't like about yourself.

There may be things that block the path between the two souls, it may be a location difference, age difference or one of the twins may already be married or partnered to someone else.

Many beautiful Twin Soul relationships do exist and do last for a lifetime. The Twin Soul relationship may be in a person's life in the form of a friend or family member, there may not need to be the sexual intimacy with your Twin Soul this life.

We have each met many Twin Souls who have moved past the need for sexual intimacy with their Twin Soul in this life. They have a higher purpose together spiritually which takes on the leading role in their relationship.

Some key examples of lessons to be learnt in a Twin Soul Mate relationship are:

- To gain deeper spiritual understanding and growth
- To be able to see the mirror side of yourself and deal with any issues that arise from that
- To enjoy a unique spiritual connection with another person physically, spiritually and mentally
- How to give and receive unconditional love

In the following case study you will see what happens when an ordinary, suburban housewife finds herself caught up in a whirlwind of emotions as she unexpectedly comes in contact with her Twin Soul.

TWIN SOUL MATES – TRACEY*

(*Names changed for privacy reasons)

Tracey came into the office looking dishevelled and much older than her forty years. She had come to the office to find some answers, her whole life was in a tail-spin and she did not know which way to turn.

During the reading it was revealed that she has been married to a lovely man for almost twenty years and they had two children who she adored. She was going through a tough time because, unexpectedly, she had met a man who had changed her whole view on life itself. Tracey was not unhappy in her marriage and she definitely was not looking for another partner or to have an affair.

It was just that, as Tracey herself expressed it, her life had gone from black and white to colour within a short amount of time. All of her thoughts were consumed by this man; she could not concentrate on her home life or feel herself connecting with her husband any more. As each day went by the connection with this new man became more and more intense. The feelings that they shared went beyond the physical sensations of lust and attraction; it was more of a spiritual and physical bonding. They would communicate via phone, text and email as much as they could without being caught out by her husband or family members.

The world which had been stable and happy and had made Tracey feel content, slowly began to feel lifeless and insignificant. She began to wonder why she would have so much of a connection with the new man if she was meant to be with her husband. It took all of Tracey's strength each morning not to pack her bags and run to be with the man.

All rational thoughts and feelings about her home life, her children and husband went out the window. Her body ached and felt hot whenever she was near the new man or even thought about him and vice versa for him. Her mind was scrambled; it felt like she was losing her mind. This is why she came for a reading to try and find some clarity to her situation.

During the reading, Tracey was able to see that this new man was indeed her Twin Soul. After discussing Twin Souls and going through the different life lessons involved with them, Tracey began to see the light turn on. Just because she had met her Twin Soul and felt all of these intense emotions it did not mean she had to leave her husband to be with him.

Tracey could still be happy, fulfilled and enjoy a long-lasting fruitful relationship with her husband, if she could see what the Twin Soul Mate relationship was for, why he had come into her life and what she needed to learn from it.

When she left the office Tracey still had a lot of soul searching to do, but now she had the knowledge she needed to decide whether she wanted to risk everything she has built in her life, her children, her family and her home for a man that had just recently come into her life.

Romantic Soul Mates

This kind of Soul Mate relationship appears a lot in the traditional fairytales and movies – some famous examples are Cinderella and her Prince, Beauty and the Beast, Robin Hood and Maid Marian.

Romantic Soul Mates are, as the name suggests, a Soul Mate that is in a romantic intimate sexual relationship with you

There is a definite purpose that brings a Romantic Soul Mate into your life – synchronicity or certain events are planned before you are born to bring you together. A Romantic Soul Mate will enter your life to help you achieve your goals of learning commitment, unconditional love or to help you to become a parent.

The Romantic Soul Mate will often feel very familiar to you when you first meet, even if you have never met them before in this life. There will be a feeling of electricity or sexual chemistry when you are with the person.

If you were to mix a Companion and Karmic Soul Mate it would often result in a Romantic Soul Mate relationship.

Some key examples of lessons to be learnt in a Romantic Soul Mate relationship are:

• To have an intimate sexual relationship which may produce children and a family
• To have a deep sense of security, friendship and trust in a relationship
• To enjoy a strong physical and spiritual connection with a partner
• How to love, support and encourage a partner for a longer term.

An important note: You can have all of the above in a Romantic Soul Mate connection, however, this isn't Hollywood, so don't expect that the road will always be smooth! You still have to work at this kind of soul connection and you'll be given some great tools to banish poor behaviours in the next section.

ROMANTIC SOUL MATES – LOUIS AND SAMANTHA

Often it will take time for Romantic Soul Mates to get together or to get through obstacles, but when they do they are usually rewarded with long-lasting rewarding relationships

Louis and Samantha met when they were teenagers. They both felt an instant attraction to each other, they felt as if they had known each other before but were not sure what it was or what it meant. They had a big group of school friends who all hung around together; they enjoyed a great friendship full of fun and typical teenage activities.

Louis and Samantha did not date each other, preferring to keep their relationship as a friendship, and as they got older, the group they hung around started to split apart as each person went their separate ways. Samantha and Louis also went down their own separate life paths, and they rarely saw each other.

At one point though, Louis was very seriously dating a girl but could not stop thinking about Samantha and wondering what she was doing and if she was OK. He would try and make contact with her but a lot of time had passed and she had moved on and was not able to be found.

Samantha was very busy working and dating a guy who was very nice, but she did not feel the same spark that she felt when she was around Louis. She wondered if Louis was happy, if he was married and if she should try and find him.

Well, as it often happens in Soul Mate relationships, a synchronistic event brought Samantha and Louis back together. They were both invited to a friend's engagement party.

The attraction, the burning sensations and the feeling of complete happiness that they both felt in each other's company was as strong as ever. They were both drawn to each other instantly and spent most of the night by themselves in the corner catching up on lost time, smiling and feeling happy to be together once again.

Louis had recently ended his relationship with his girlfriend and Samantha had been on the brink of breaking up with her boyfriend for months. That night it was made very clear that they both had strong feelings for each other which were definitely more than friendship.

Samantha decided to end her relationship with her boyfriend the next day. Both Louis and Samantha knew it felt right to be together. They were inseparable after their friend's engagement party. Within six months they were engaged themselves and within another six months their first child was already on the way.

Louis and Samantha ended up getting married, having a child and living the life that each had been looking for with other people. This is a good example of a Romantic Soul Mate relationship because it highlights that there is a deep feeling of connection and/or a physical attraction which does not fade away easily.

Synchronistic events do bring Soul Mates together a lot of the time because we pre-plan who we want to meet and what we want to learn before we are born. Free will is important as you ultimately choose your own life path, but if you need any extra help the Universe likes to give you a helping hand, hence the synchronicity.

WHY WE GET INTO TROUBLE ... THE MISIDENTIFICATION OF SOUL MATES

The whole idea of Soul Mates is very appealing to most people, whether they admit it or not. To be able to find a person who will complete us and be everything we have ever dreamed of – best friend, lover, confidante – Who wouldn't be interested in that?

We often see people reaching and searching for their one and only Soul Mate. Trying to find value in their life, happiness and fulfilment, so who can blame them for pinning all their hopes on another soul!

It can be a big order to fill though, trying to fit all of our hopes and dreams into one person, one Soul Mate. Once you are aware that there are different types of Soul Mates in your life you can begin to take the pressure of yourself and see each relationship or connection for what it is.

Where we can all get into trouble is by misidentifying our Soul Mate relationships. It can be like trying to fit a square peg into a round hole. If you are trying to make a Karmic relationship a long lasting Romantic relationship it won't work, nor will a Companion relationship fulfil the role of an intense Twin Soul relationship – they are completely different.

We may try to push for an intimate relationship or wait in hope that it will turn into an intimate relationship when the connection is only meant to be a Companion Soul Mate – or maybe not even a Soul Mate relationship at all! This can lead to disappointment and even resentment of the other when they fail to fulfil our expectations. Worse still, we can completely miss the benefits of having them in our lives because we are looking for them to be or do something different.

We would like to make it easier for you to tell the difference between Soul Mate relationships so you have the best chance of achieving happiness in whatever relationships you have.

We have prepared a convenient table comparing the different kinds of Soul Mates. We invite you to look at the table below and focus on a particular person in your life that you would like to know more about.

On the chart you will notice that we have provided you with some suggestions on how you might feel when you encounter these people. We suggest that you get a piece of paper and write down which of the emotions best describes how you feel when you think of that person and then match it to the chart below.

Although you may feel a mixture of emotions about this person and this may well go across a number of Soul Mate types, there will be one that will stand out, if you are honest.

SOUL MATE CHARACTERISTICS CHART

Soul Mate Type	Relationship Type	Positive Feelings	Shadow Feelings	Physical Feelings
Karmic	Ex Partner/ Lover	Passion Intimacy (not always) Excitement	Vulnerability Volatility Fear Desperation Guilt Unfinished Business (if lesson has not been learnt)	Heat, Chemistry, Sexual Attraction or Repulsion
	Boss / Co-worker	Personal Strength Independence	Confusion Fear	
	Family Member	Forgiveness Love	Isolation Repression	
	Friend/Ex Friend	Spontaneity Courage	Anger Frustration	
	Teacher	Knowledge Trust	Loss Despair	
Companion	Friend	Companionship Communication Support Compassion Like Minded	Frustration Confusion	Lack of Sexual Intimacy
	Family Member	Love Trust	Co-dependence	

Soul Mate Type	Relationship Type	Positive Feelings	Shadow Feelings	Physical Feelings
	Pet	Loyalty Security		
	Teacher	Stability Self Expression		
	Acquaintance	Knowledge Connection		
Twin	Lover	Telepathic Link Deep Spiritual Connection, Equality Increased Psychic Awareness, Past Life Recall Feeling Complete Security Love Spontaneity Sense of Purpose	Confusion Frustration Fear Desperation Guilt Yearning Jealousy Lack of Control Volatility Anger Vulnerability	Intense physical feelings: heat, scattered mind, heightened sexual attraction

Soul Mate Type	Relationship Type	Positive Feelings	Shadow Feelings	Physical Feelings
Twin (cont.)	Friend	Telepathic Link Deep Spiritual Connection, Equality Increased Psychic Awareness, Past Life Recall Sense of Purpose Feeling Complete Security Love	Jealousy Frustration Confusion	No Sexual Attraction or Intimacy
Romantic	Lover/ Partner	Stability Intimacy Sense of Purpose Love Security	Frustration Repression Vulnerability Fear	Sexual Attraction, Chemistry to Reproduce Offspring

In the table you can clearly see that there are various feelings or emotions that can cross over from each type of Soul Mate relationship. This can confuse us and make us wonder just which type of relationship we are in.

Perseverance is the key.

It can sometimes be horrifying to work out that the person that you have had your heart set on is actually not (and never will be) a Romantic Soul Mate. This happens all the time!

It is a very common situation that people are friends and one likes the idea of taking it further and being more romantic. The other person couldn't comprehend being intimate with that person and they love the friendship only. These cases of unrequited love can go on for years and years. What a waste! Hollywood is king of this scenario. There are so many movies where one person (normally a man) loves a woman more gorgeous than him and she only sees him as the geeky friend. She is dating some hot, but bad, guy and she eventually sees the geek for his amazing qualities and falls for him, after which they live happily ever after.

Do you know how rare this is? Do you understand that in real life, if she did end up with him it's probably because she has been hurt that one too many times and she is settling for a companion Soul Mate! What's more, she is more likely to realise down the track that, because of the lack of passionate, sexual chemistry, this really isn't enough for her and will go off having affairs.

Now wouldn't it have been prudent ... although hard admittedly, to identify that the one-sided relationship that you are having is just that ... one sided! By ending that false obsession you save years of angst, drama and misdirected energy. We cannot tell you how awful it is for us to see this situation occurring over and over, in particular with women in their mid to late 30s onwards. These women finally wake up to the fact that the man or men they have been focussing on really are not Romantic Soul Mates but Companion (or Karmic) and they feel they have missed the boat for childbearing.

Try not to be too hard on yourself if you have made a mistake and have misidentified a relationship. None of us are perfect. We have all had times in our lives where we may have tried to make something out of a relationship that wasn't really there.

You may have had a purely physical relationship or you may have just misread the feelings and signs that you experienced. That is ok, it is all about learning and growing and enjoying yourself in the process.

But it has to stop there.

If you are not in the kind of Soul Mate relationship that you want to be, don't worry, it's not all doom and gloom. Each person is different and each person needs to learn things in their own way. However we know that you would prefer not to have to learn the same thing over and over. Wouldn't it be better to be able to identify your lesson more quickly and accurately, then act upon this in a suitable way, without unnecessary pain over long periods?

Aren't you over wasting your time?

IDENTIFYING YOUR SOUL MATE CONNECTION
LUSTY ONE NIGHT STAND OR ... ?

Every day in our consultancies we encounter truly smart, interesting and seemingly quite self aware people who are making huge mistakes in love. This is certainly not a deliberate choice ... who in their right mind would direct themselves into more pain, more confusion, more heartache?

Some of our clients have it so bad that they have even given up on the whole love thing entirely, their hearts burnt to a crisp, never again to be filled with the delicious lifeblood of love.

But it doesn't have to be this way.

How would you feel if we could give you some hints and tips that would make choosing and keeping a partner easier and less painful?

How would you feel if you could accurately and quickly recognise what kind of soul mate was in front of you and make an informed decision about what to do next?

We would like to let you in on some dating and relationship secrets, tell-tale signs and emotions that you may be overlooking. These signs can help you to classify what kind of Soul Mate relationship it is and therefore how you should treat it.

THE BIG INDICATOR IS HOW WE FEEL.

The way we feel gives us a big clue as to whether it is a short term Karmic relationship, a Companion, a Twin Soul or if it is indeed a longer term Romantic Soul Mate relationship.

> 'A soul mates purpose is to shake you up, tear apart your ego a little bit, show you your obstacles and addictions, break your heart open so new light can get in, make you so desperate and out of control that you have to transform your life...'

Eat, Pray, Love One Woman's Search for Everything, Bloomsbury Publishing, London 2006.

Elizabeth Gilbert

Elizabeth Gilbert's quote uses words like 'shake you up', 'tear apart', 'desperate and out of control'. These are the extreme kind of emotions that can often be felt in Twin or Karmic Soul Mate relationships.

Jamie, a 28-year-old accountant from New York explained his relationship like this:

'When I met her I thought I had been run over by a bus. I couldn't keep her out of my mind, I wanted to call her all the time. And when we did speak half the time we were fighting or debating. Then we would have make-up sex or break up, and then the cycle would start all over again. She felt the same way. I would know when she was going to call. Just thinking about her would make me physically burn and she told me a similar thing.

This was so weird for me. I am a typical mild mannered accountant. But if you had told me to run naked across the country just to see her, I would have done it.'

We can rejoice for or pity Jamie. He has certainly encountered some kind of Soul Mate here, but what kind? Is it a potentially destructive relationship or just the simple ebb and flow of a Romantic connection? By being able to identify the difference, Jamie is able to make a decision about whether to stay or leave.

The way that Jamie can identify what kind of Soul Mate he has encountered is to surgically examine how he feels, and then he can make a decision on how long he wants to stay in this relationship in order to move forward spiritually.

Jamie feels quite an obsession – extreme lustful emotion – and there is a high degree of volatility. He also feels quite a lot of confusion and frustration at his own behaviour. He doesn't understand his own irrationality.

Now we could say, sure it's the love drugs running around in his body that is turning him into a crazy man. And that is probably part of it … but not all of it.

If we look at these 'symptoms' they describe a certain kind of Soul Mate pretty clearly. They identify a **Twin Soul Mate**.

How do you think you would feel if you met your Twin Soul? Typically the emotions that you would encounter would be extreme and intense. For example:

- Extreme Lust and Passion (which could lead to stalking or obsession)
- Frustration
- Fear
- Anger
- Jealousy
- Confusion
- Volatility

- Compulsive behaviour with little concern for consequences
- Feeling connected spiritually and physically

Now, knowing the nature of this relationship, being forewarned about what it is, Jamie can be better prepared to deal with the consequences of staying or going.

When you begin to look at your relationships, past and present, it is imperative to look at emotions and feelings FIRST.

For example, are you sexually attracted to the person? Do you want to leap into bed with them and have rampant sex? Or would you rather sit on the couch and happily watch a DVD with them?

Do you feel happy and alive when you are with them … but also without them?

Do you feel secure and confident or edgy and distracted?

Do you feel obsessive or a pleasant hum of connection?

If you wake up in the morning after a one night stand and would rather chew your own arm off rather than wake them up ... it's probably not the love of your life but something else!

To discern properly, you need to be aware of your own emotions.

This means, we need to be aware of how we feel in the moment, in real time.

This requires a good level of knowledge of oneself and an awareness of emotional intelligence. This can be challenging and takes practice and time. Later in this book, we give you some excellent tools to assist you to build some self knowledge, self esteem and self trust, which are all imperative to a rounded sense of emotional intelligence.

ROMANTIC VS. TWIN SOUL MATE CONNECTION

Because of the intense connection, synchronicity of events and sense of recognition when you first meet, it can be difficult to tell the difference between a Romantic Soul Mate and a Twin Soul connection.

A difference between the Twin and Romantic Soul Mates is that a Twin Soul Mate relationship can be quite difficult to withstand a long duration of time in the relationship, because of the intensity of emotions and lessons between the Twin Souls. Within a Romantic Soul Mate relationship it can be easier to last the distance of time in the relationship if the two Soul Mates choose to. Remember, the key discerning factor is the level of intensity and volatility.

Below is a questionnaire which can be used to help you to tell the difference between a Romantic and Twin Soul relationship.

TWIN vs. ROMANTIC SOUL MATE QUESTIONAIRE 1

1. Have you ever felt a strong instant physical or telepathic connection with the other person? Yes or No
2. Have you felt an intense burning of need and desire to be with the other person, even if it isn't realistic or socially acceptable? Yes or No
3. Do you feel as if you are on a natural high (state of ecstasy) when you are with the other person, either physically or mentally? Yes or No
4. Is it extremely emotionally painful for you to be apart from the other person physically and/or mentally? Yes or No
5. Does your body heat up, burn or feel energetically a lot different when you are around the other person's energy? Yes or No
6. Can you physically feel when the other person is thinking of you and vice versa? Yes or No
7. Have you and the other person remembered some of your past lives together? Yes or No
8. Has your spiritual knowledge and understanding increased since meeting this person and vice versa? Yes or No

9. Are you finding it difficult to stay grounded and focused on your normal everyday life? Yes or No
10. Is the pull to the other person so strong that you would give up many things that are currently in your life just to be with the other person? Yes or No

If you answered YES to five or more of the questions below you have met your Twin Soul Mate. If you answered YES to three to four questions you have met a Romantic Soul Mate.

Which Soul Mate connection is it?

If you have experienced some of the following scenarios you have encountered a Soul Mate relationship:

• A synchronistic event will bring you together.
• You may have similar interests or lived in similar areas for most of your life. There will be too many similarities for it to be coincidental

For example both of us have husbands who are called Adam, both of our Adams love the ocean and surfing, both have dark hair and are quite tall … the list goes on. We also both have similar interests. This kind of similarity is typical with Soul Mates, including Companion Soul Mates and we are definitely that.

• You have an intense like or dislike of the other person's energy

For example have you ever felt an intense dislike for someone instantly? It can feel as if all the hairs stand up on your arms (hopefully not your back). Your stomach feels tight as you get yourself ready for a physical battle. It's almost an antibody reaction.

• You are able to communicate freely and easily with each other.

For example you can tell them the truth about what they are wearing and vice versa, without having to think about it too much, 'Seriously those black fish net stockings really don't suit you!'

- An intense physical attraction: you feel as if you may explode or implode just being near them.

ASK YOURSELF ...

Here are some questions that will make it clearer for you to decide what kind of Soul Mate relationship you are in:

- Do I feel sexually attracted to the other person or am I just trying to settle with someone in case I don't find someone else?
- Is there an intense telepathic connection, do you call each other on the phone at the same time or feel when each other are in pain?
- Do you feel like you have known this person before, even though you have never met them previously in this life?
- What is your physical behaviour around this person? Do you feel like you just want to hang out with them or do you want to be more intimate? Is there a particular thing you are drawn to doing with them – a certain sport, travelling, music – but not much else?

Moving forward with Knowledge

Now that you have seen that there are a number of distinct types of Soul Mates, you can identify what you have attracted into your life far faster and more accurately. The benefits of this are many.

For starters, having this practical knowledge will enable you to make better decisions about who you wish to invite into your life and enable you to stop wasting your valuable time on people who will never be the kind of Soul Mate that you are after.

This wisdom also enables you to reduce the misguided need to settle for someone who isn't quite right. You can move forward with confidence and a joyous lightness that perhaps you haven't felt in some time.

SECTION 2

OBSTACLE BUSTING – GETTING RID OF THE BARRIERS IN YOUR WAY

Chances are some of you are reading this book because you have been trying to find that ideal Soul Mate connection and are frustrated by the lack of success. You have tried to draw a new relationship and you don't understand why it isn't coming together, why those around you seem to fall into happy relationships so easily, yet it still eludes you.

Now you know how to clearly identify and differentiate the different types of Soul Mate connections now is the time to look at the things which may be working against your intentions.

WHAT'S IN THE WAY ... US!

If you have found the process of creating a happy, healthy relationship difficult in the past, no doubt you will now want to find a Romantic Soul Mate pretty quickly, with as little fuss and pain as possible. But before you can do this you need to identify why your efforts have not worked in the past.

To do this, we need you to get extremely tough with yourself and take personal responsibility for your share of what has happened in past relationships. This search for that great Romantic Soul Mate is all about YOU and the action YOU choose to take from this second onwards.

Hang on.

Maybe you go out lots, do everything possible but still don't meet anyone worthwhile … how can that be your fault?

What about what your last boyfriend did to you, or your evil ex-wife who scarred you forever?

What about the abusive guy who verbally and physically attacked you, surely that wasn't your fault at all?

Of course it isn't your *fault*. This is not about fault. This is not about apportioning blame. This is not about being a victim or a martyr. What this is about is you taking responsibility for your part and then letting the past go. Holding on to anything but the wisdom you have gained through relationships that haven't worked is an obstacle. By removing obstacles, by changing our negative beliefs, we lighten our load and we begin to enjoy our lives more fully. We automatically have more flow and begin to attract what we want … in this case a red hot smokin' Soul Mate!

There are several obstacle-busting techniques which will help you break these patterns and release and transform these belief systems. The first is to openly and honestly look at the things which can hinder these efforts to bring a positive Soul Mate connection in.

So let's start the process of getting out of our own way, shall we?

FLUSHING OUT THE SOUL MONSTERS

How can you stop re-enacting the same situations and relationships that keep causing you unhappiness? How can you take control back and start having the relationships that you want?

It's easier than you think, but you have to be willing to start by addressing the following three things:

One: Reject Denial

Be aware that you have played a part in where you are right now. Acknowledge that there may be some hidden unconscious beliefs and that it's worth finding them. Denial gets you nowhere.

CONSCIOUS VERSUS UNCONSCIOUS BELIEFS

How we think and how we feel has a major impact on what we draw to us or choose to invite into our lives. Most of us think we know what we are thinking, that we control our thoughts, and that is true, up to a point. We can recognise and thus more easily control our conscious thoughts, the beliefs and ideas we know we have. To do this we just need to analyse our thoughts and consider our actions. However there is another set of soul monsters lurking and these are the beliefs that we don't know we have … the unconscious ones.

Just like it can take time for trust to build up in relationships, it can take time for us to realise the nature of the connections we have with other people.

Often we are not consciously aware of what we are attracting.

Our belief systems are put into place in our early formative years, as young as three years old. They assist us with structure, boundaries and meaning as we grow, and enable us to work within our society. As much as we may hate to admit it, these early belief systems do dramatically affect the way we live in our adult lives. Some of these beliefs are deeply ingrained and we see life through the filter of them.

Having beliefs is not a bad thing – our belief systems give our life meaning and help us to know who we are and what to make out of our life. What is limiting is if we have beliefs, either consciously or unconsciously, which can be hurtful to us.

Let us give you an example or two.

If you are living in Western Culture, you are reaching or passing the age of 40, are female and still haven't found a satisfying Romantic Soul Mate, you may, through your own set of belief filters and through what you perceive is society's beliefs, come to the conclusion that you are too old to attract a sexy man and will never be a mother.

Without going into the statistics (and the evidence of a number of gorgeous pregnant plus 40s in our offices) this is not a true statement. That is not to say you can't justify this statement, you may have this belief because of a wide variety of influencing factors – the media, what Mum said at her 40th birthday party, the scales showing the added 5 kilos since last year – but because the belief is justified doesn't mean it is true. The only thing that creates truth of a belief is the belief in it. Once you believe it is true then the brain, the body and, if you are so inclined, The Universe, sees it as truth too. And thus it becomes truth in all its consequences.

This negative self talk will manifest negative consequences, yet most of the time we are completely unaware that it is us creating the things we do not want. Unconscious negative self talk is so powerful because we do not even know we are doing it. It's elusive, changeble – one day you might think 'I look great!' and the next 'Geez! I look terrible'. Your mood, attitude and actions will match the positive thoughts and the negative, just as effectively.

We have all engaged in some negative self talk at some stage in our lives. When we talk to ourselves in a negative way, it is often the result of our own unconscious, unresolved past hurts and the beliefs that come from these.

Have you ever heard of the old saying 'Like attracts like?' If we are talking negatively to ourselves consciously or unconsciously we will be more likely to expect and attract a negative experience. This can mean we actually stop or slow the process of attraction.

Here are some further examples of negative unconscious self talk from some of our clients:

Mark believes that he is too skinny, ugly, boring – destined to be single and alone forever. Teased at school for being smaller than the other boys and naturally more introverted, Mark began to form this nasty set of beliefs because he didn't really have the internal resources to stand solid and know who he really was and that the real him was OK.

Who he really is, amongst other positive things, is an interesting, thoughtful, intellectually bright guy with great brown eyes and a sweet smile. Because of his beliefs though, Mark had made a self fulfilling prophecy. He has never been in a long-term intimate loving relationship. Mark's belief has become his reality because he is unconsciously focussing on those negative aspects and attracting those experiences of that lonely life.

Mark doesn't make an effort in his physical appearance; he shies away from any social interaction and is distant emotionally. His hermit-like existence does not give him the opportunity to meet anyone. He hasn't even had a chance of a date or a sexual relationship because he really just does not involve himself in life.

It's not that Mark is physically unattractive, it is the energy or, in this case, lack of energy he is unconsciously putting out to other people – we ladies really don't dig guys who are totally invisible, don't ever make eye contact or spend time trying to hide behind the office photocopier at lunch time. We need something which catches our eye or heart to makes us feel physically or emotionally attracted.

We are not saying that everyone needs to look like Brad or Angelina. We are saying that there does need to be some spark or some physical presence that makes people stop and take notice long enough for you to meet them or interact with them. This is about confidence and charisma (from the Greek meaning the spirit shining through), not about having model looks.

Here is another example of unconscious limiting behaviour caused by negative beliefs:

Chrissie is an attractive, vibrant, successful lady who continues to unconsciously attract men into her life who cheat on her and disrespect her. She has had an unconscious belief system that no one would want to be in a monogamous, long-lasting loving relationship with her.

Her belief systems have been formed since she was a little girl, after being constantly told that she was not good enough, not pretty enough, that no one would ever want her and that she is worthless.

Chrissie was aware of some of her unconscious belief systems; she had smashed through the emotional hurts connected to feeling unattractive and worthless in most areas of her life. She has become an extremely successful businesswoman, she loves the way she looks and has loads of friends to have fun with.

But Chrissie has not managed to break through that negative opinion of herself in her relationship area. Chrissie is unconsciously attracting men who are already married or attached in a relationship. She doesn't go out looking for an attached man, it just happens that way. These men want to wine and dine Chrissie, they want to hook up with her for late night booty calls – but they always end up going back to their wives or partners.

Chrissie only attracts 'unavailable' men. She is always the 'other woman'.

Chrissie's unconscious belief of her worthlessness is dominant in her attract-ive energy. By believing deep down that that no one would really want to be in a monogamous, long-lasting relationship with her, she settles for sharing. Sure, she hopes that she can eventually convince them that she is the 'better' woman but the guys she dates are the kind that are happy to have their cake and eat it too. Chrissie believes that the kind of quality man she truly seeks would never be interested in someone as worthless as she is, so she is never attracted to them. It's just safer that way.

When we consciously or unconsciously 'buy in' to a belief, we make it absolute truth for us and act upon it continually, the results are then often a frustrating pattern that our conscious selves don't understand.

Two: Be Completely Honest

Pay attention to the types of people or situations you are habitually attracting. Look with a scrupulously honest eye at what is making you unhappy in your life and the relationships or the kind of person that is. You may wish to get a trusted outside opinion from a friend or professional just in case you do indeed have a blind-spot that is side-swiping you.

It certainly can be a daunting experience looking back over our past relationship hurts, but it is essential to do this. The only way you can move forward in your life is by shining a torch on all of the monsters (unconscious beliefs) which are under your bed or in the big scary relationship closet. We then can take steps to remove and transform these beliefs and patterns giving us a clear run at what we do want.

PATTERNS

Have you ever said to a friend 'I can't believe it? Why do I keep meeting these terrible men/women?'

Has a friend ever said to you 'You'll love this person; they are exactly the type you go for.'

Have you ever thought 'Oh my god, the same thing happened as last time!'

Have you ever broken up with someone and realised that you broke up with them for exactly the same reason as you broke up with the last one.

Have you ever had a negative phone call with your boy/girlfriend and thought 'It's happening AGAIN! Why didn't I see this coming?'

We have got news for you … if it feels like relationship groundhog day; you have a relationship pattern going on!

Now, some patterns are positive. These patterns are the things that benefit you and are strategies that serve you well. Say, a pattern that enables you to attract solid friendships or continual prosperity in your business.

Unfortunately, some are negative, our repeated soul monsters if you like, and these are the ones we want to expose and hunt down.

Often, we see our friends and family members making the same mistakes over and over again by attracting the same type of partner and going through the same kind of drama and hurtful experiences. We can see it oh-so-clearly and want so much for them to see it too. As we sit back and watch we can see from the outside what is going on and can see that a pattern is repeating and we know what will come next. We can do this because we have some distance, perspective – and it's not us!

From the safety of distance, we may ponder, 'Why does she stay with that guy when he treats her so badly? Sure, he may be all right to look at but why, oh why does she stay? This happened with the last one!'

Sometimes people may be so caught up in the lust or deep emotional beliefs from this life or a past life that they can't see that they are caught in a never ending cycle of similar life lessons. These lessons never seem to be resolved, even though the partners have changed; the lessons keep on reappearing and repeating themselves.

While providing readings and consultations we often see clients who come to us wanting to find Mr or Mrs Right. They want to move forward with their lives but they can't seem to put their finger on what is going wrong for them in their relationship area.

The first question we often ask them is: 'What has been going wrong for you?'

They reveal their story and, through its twists and turns, usually a pattern is revealed and the person is either oblivious to it or just doesn't know why it keeps happening.

We then go on to help them identify their past hurts and the beliefs that may not serve them. We show them what they have been manifesting is a result of what intentions they have been putting out. This is often shocking to them, but a huge relief as well, because now they are armed with the information to begin to stop the pattern.

Another common scenario that exposes the presence of a pattern (positive or negative) is people that are attracted to an easily identifiable type.

Are you interested in only one type of personality? Always the 'bad boy' or always the 'shy guy'. Maybe it's the 'party girl' or the 'submissive one?'

In the instance of physical appearances, have a look back on the type of guys or girls you are usually physically attracted to. Is there a common theme in their physical appearances? Do they have always have similar hair or eye colouring, body type; are they of a similar height?

The key here is the word *always*. If you *always* do something, it is a pattern.

It's important to have a long, hard, conscious look to whether that pattern is benefiting you or limiting you. If it's something that limits you, then it needs to go … with no excuses!

Belief Systems Exercise

So as you can see there are many belief systems which influence the way we see the world. Many of our fears or hurts may have come from our current life or they may have even come from our previous lives.

It doesn't matter which life the pain is coming from, the important thing is that we bust through the obstacles and move on. It's important to set ourselves free and to move on so that we can be happy, fulfilled and full of energy and life … which you will see later is a key way to attract the Soul Mate you want faster.

We invite you to do the following exercise and answer the following questions. Make the answers concise and honest. We often think point form is a good way of doing this. Take your time doing this but don't overthink your answers. As we said earlier, should you wish to have a trusted friend comment on some of your answers, please do.

Go somewhere private. Light a candle to assist your focus. Breathe deeply and pay attention to your breath until you are more centered.

Answer these questions as fully yet concisely as possible:

When it comes to relationships I am afraid of …

I dislike these things about myself …

I am most afraid of people finding out the following about me …

Based on my past experiences, I think the most negative part of being in a relationship is …

I have a type I prefer. This is it: (e.g. tall dark handsome, party boy/girl, quiet type etc)

I am most uncomfortable in a relationship when …

These are the family beliefs I carry about love and relationships …

These are my big doubts about this process …

If you already know some of your negative patterns or beliefs add them here too:

What is my biggest barrier to experiencing more pleasure in my life?

Is there a relationship with a person, past or present that I feel I can't quite get over?

Now some of these answers may be a surprise, some pleasant and some just disappointments ... but either way, you should be celebrating. You have set a successful trap for this lot of soul monsters and now we can remove them for good.

Belief Systems from Past Lives
A HAREM OR A CONVENT ...

Sometimes the reason that people can make the same relationship mistakes over and over again is because of beliefs and experiences that come from an unexpected place ... your past lives!

The idea of past lives or reincarnation is a controversial one. For every deeply held belief that the soul does not die but is reborn into another physical body and another physical life, there is an equally steadfast belief that this is just new age nonsense.

The debate is worthy of a book on its own, and we don't intend to discuss it here and now, all we will ask is for you to have an open mind and consider whether the possibility of past lives and the consequences they could carry may be something that can help you solve difficulties in this life.

Let's imagine that our source self ... or soul ... is placed in a physical vessel, our body. For the soul, it's like wearing a jacket. We wear this jacket and it may get some wear, and tear a few rips and stains and eventually it becomes too tight and small. We outwear or outgrow the jacket when we die and our soul self is free to then choose another physical vessel or jacket.

This new jacket could be bright and shiny and modern, but our soul source may remember the last jacket. Its fit, its positives and its stains and tears. So, there is some residual memory of the last jacket.

So bringing this back to our lives now, what happened to us in our previous lives - particularly the extreme things – emotions, loves, hurts, injuries, obsessions – which could affect our current life because of this residual memory.

So what does this look or feel like?

A past life preference can manifest in a number of ways. Often people are unconsciously drawn to or attracted to a particular personality trait or physical appearance.

We all are born with certain likes or dislikes, things that make us feel attracted or repulsed. A lot of our likes and dislikes are not only from what we have experienced in our present life, sometimes they are brought forth from the past lives. This means that many times our past life likes and dislikes will affect our current life without us even realising the source.

Let's look at an example:

Jacinta has always preferred tall men with long, dark hair and olive skin. This has been since she was a child. No one in her family looks like this. She also enjoys males who are highly physical and protective with a warrior-like attitude.

As Jacinta grew older she saw images of Native American warriors in books and documentaries and was immediately attracted to them. As an adult many years later, she eventually travelled to the United States and encountered Native American people. There was an immediate sense of recognition and belonging. She felt at home in a way she had never felt before. She had never felt that kind of intensity in her native country and had difficulty in connecting with Anglo-Saxon men. She began a relationship with a Native American man and the connection was both physically and spiritually satisfying.

We identified with Jacinta that one of her past lives was as a Native American woman. Her preference for that particular physical type, when she had no exposure previously, was a big clue. More so, her attraction to the personality type of the warrior and the overwhelmingly positive sensations around the culture and her sense of belonging was an even stronger link.

We may also have our own strong belief systems or vows that we have taken in past lives. These beliefs or vows can subconsciously affect the way we think about our relationships in this life.

In the case studies below, you will see how looking at who or what you believed in past lives can definitely give you some clues as to why you are attracting or acting the way you do in this life.

FRANK – THE SULTAN

An example of this is a client that came to the office; Frank was a very well-dressed man who was quite successful in his own business, yet he couldn't seem to find happiness with a long-lasting relationship. He wanted to know why he seemed to only constantly feel the need to date a number of women at the same time, despite the fact that he really wanted to find one genuine, faithful relationship.

Each time he met a nice woman and thought she could be the one he could be monogamous with, maybe even marry and have kids with, he would find himself being attracted to another woman. It was a compulsion. The other woman was always someone that didn't fit the right mould for a wife and kids; she was an escape, a lust partner. This pattern would repeat and repeat causing constant drama and upset in his relationships.

Looking into his past lives and relationships, a very common theme came through. Frank had a pattern of having many wives and/or partners in each life. In one of his most successful and powerful lives he was a sultan, with his own harem of wives from which he was able to pick and choose who and when he wanted.

In that life, Frank did have a favourite wife who was quite young and had given birth to a son for him. This wife was very beautiful, but was not treated very well by the other wives in the harem. She became quite ill and was left to fend for herself.

Frank, who as the sultan could not be seen to favour her, did little to specifically help this wife and as a result she ended up dying quite quickly. The Sultan was heartbroken; he never got to say goodbye to his young wife. Because of his grief and loss he vowed to never have his heart set on just one wife again.

By looking back at this past life Frank recognised the patterns in his current life. He would panic and push the women away who were suitable and who he was falling in love with. His cell memory was thinking that he had to have many partners so that he wouldn't have to experience that loss and heartbreak again.

It was important for him to cut the cords and patterns from that past life so that he could sustain a long lasting, loving, monogamous relationship in this life.

As you can see sometimes we are not only drawn to particular personality traits or patterns in our relationships, we may also have our own belief systems or vows that we have taken in past lives which can subconsciously affect the way we think about relationships in this life.

JUDY (THE NUN)

Judy walked into the office quietly, trying not to disturb anyone; she was a petite little woman with shoulder length mousy brown hair. She walked over and sat down on the couch. As she was sitting down, Judy began to fidget and looked extremely uncomfortable.

After a few minutes she began to explain she wanted to know why she couldn't bring herself to be in a relationship with a man and why she was so unsuccessful in finding an intimate partner.

After Judy relaxed a bit more we discussed how sometimes our past lives can affect our current lives. Judy was interested in this concept and so we began to look at some of her past lives.

Just like in Frank's case study, there was a very significant common theme which kept appearing in Judy's lives. Judy had so many lifetimes being of service to the community, the church, the monastery, the temple or the hospital. She had given all of her life to everyone else, her time and her passion were all caught up in her life's purpose of being of service to others.

In her past lives Judy had no opportunity to be intimate, passionate and happy in a sexual relationship. She had to spend many hours alone at night in prayer or meditation and was extremely disconnected from any physical sensations or intimacy.

Her celibate lifetimes were holding her back and making her feel guilty for wanting a physical sexual relationship in this life. Every time she felt like she was getting too serious with a man she would feel herself putting up blocks and walls and feeling guilty for even thinking of having any sexual physical interactions.

Judy's life became miserable because she felt she would have to choose between her career/life of service or an intimate relationship. She did not realise that in this life she didn't need to choose between the two, she could have both a rewarding career life and a loving intimate relationship.

Once Judy realised that the past was holding her back, we were able to cut the celibate bonds from her past lives – something that we explain fully in the last section of this book. She was then more able to move forward into a passionate, loving relationship with a man while still maintaining her career and life's passion for helping others.

TIM – THE KARMIC SWITCH

Tim, a tall, well-built man in his mid thirties, came into the office for a reading. He was dressed nicely; had sandy blond hair and a cheeky smile. If anyone out in the street saw Tim they would think he was attractive and successful, living a prosperous life.

What other people didn't realise is that Tim was very unhappy in his relationship area. While having his reading it was revealed that Tim was constantly drawn to women who are aggressive, selfish, and unfaithful. There was no lack of women attracted to Tim; it was the quality of the women that was the problem.

He would meet a lady, be attracted to her energy and physical looks and think that he had found 'The One'. The relationship would go well for a few weeks and then it would all go pear shaped. The women would start to show their true colours. They would often become extremely feisty and aggressive – lashing out at Tim and blame him for things he hadn't said or done.

Sure, perhaps Tim may have done some things to annoy these women, after all it takes two to tango, but by looking back at some of Tim's past lives it began to shine a light on some of the reasons why he was attracting these kinds of women in this life.

In many of Tim's past lives he was very aggressive to his family members and partners. He would often beat his wife and make outrageous accusations against her. He was extremely jealous and this impacted not only him but his wife and children as well.

Just by looking back at some of his past lives Tim was able to see why he was drawing a similar energy to him. He was unconsciously trying to fix a karmic debt he felt he owed to his previous partners and family members.

In attracting these types of women, Tim unconsciously may feel that he can not only heal them, but also heal parts of himself from previous lives.

Tim may be trying to help heal the women and make himself feel wanted, needed and respected, because previously he was the one in the past lives that was unethical, unfaithful and extremely aggressive towards other people.

HOW CAN WE DETERMINE IF WE HAVE HAD A PAST LIFE?

There are many different ways to access your past lives:

- Conscious or subconscious daydreaming/deja vu
- Dreaming
- Meditation
- Guided meditation on CD or DVD
- Hypnosis/past life regression by a qualified professional
- Scrying with ink, crystal ball, a mirror or a pendulum
- Channelling to connect with your own intuition
- Psychic past life reading

You can access your own past lives in the privacy of your own home or by visiting a qualified past life regressionist or psychic practitioner who specialises in this.

It can be very confronting for some people to go into a strange office of a hypnotist or past life regressionist, but don't let that hold you back. It is a very powerful experience in the right hands. However, we have found that you can do the following exercise in the comfort of your own home without even having to go into a deep trance or meditation.

We would like to offer you this quick and simple exercise that will help you identify who you may have been in one of your past lives. It requires you to relax, not to think, just to pay attention to the first bit of information that comes into your head and allow it to come through.

Don't stop to think, just write down the first thing that comes into your mind. There are no right or wrong answers. If you get stuck, just relax and start over. Try not to analyse or rationalise what you are seeing, feeling or hearing, as this involves the conscious mind (very much a 'this life' tool).

Quick and Simple Past Life Exercise

YOU WILL NEED:

- A safe quiet place to lie down privately
- A notebook and a pen
- **Optional**: Calming music

Relax now and ask for The Universe to surround you in a bubble of protective white light.

Breathe deeply and think of a pleasant place or experience for you.

When you are feeling safe and positive, ask for your most important past life to be shown to you.

The following quick questions will help you to go right to your unconscious memory to give you some answers to who you were and what may have gone on in your relationships in past lives.

Remember to grab the first answer that comes into your head; don't overthink it! Write down the answer as quickly as possible, then move on to the next question immediately.

What country are you in?
Are you male or female?
Are you married, single or widowed?
How do you feel in your relationship area?
What physical looks are you attracted to?
What personality traits do you like in a partner?
Are you happy and fulfilled?
If you're not happy, why are you not happy?
Do you have any parents?
Do you have any siblings?
Do you have any children?
What is the most important thing to you in this life?
If you could change anything in that life, what would it be?

How would you change your relationships in this past life?
What are your greatest skills and joys in this life?

When you have found the answers to the above questions, take a deep breath and you can return to your present life.

Know that you are safe and protected.

It's fine if you are feeling a bit emotional; this is very normal. Write down everything that you have seen, felt or experienced.

It's important to know that you are now back in this, your present, life so a good way to ground yourself is to say your name out loud three times.

Check your answers. By looking at both the positives and the negatives of this past life you can see if they impact this life in any way.

You can make informed changes in your life now to move forward. Use the information from your past life questions to help you to see why it is that you may feel or do things either positively or negatively in your relationship area.

If there are negative impacts, please ensure you seriously consider releasing these during the obstacle-busting exercises we will be introducing to you soon.

<u>Three: Release and Transform</u>

Once you have discovered your conscious and unconscious beliefs, you need to release and transform them. You can begin to consciously work on growing positive beliefs that will replace the limiting ones you have uncovered. Transform negative habits into positive ones and replace negative self-talk and belief with positive beliefs and you will begin to attract all the aspects that you want to in your life and relationships.

If we go back to Mark's example, as soon as he realises that his beliefs about himself are not protecting but limiting him, he can begin to change the way he sees himself. As a gentle start, he may like to go out and buy some new clothes, get a new hair style or even start to go to a gym. Better still, begin to discover what it is that makes him happier. These may all sound like very superficial changes, centring around his physical looks, but actually it's more about how he sees himself and how he feels when he goes out into public. His energy will be more confident and will be much more appealing.

If Mark goes out to the gym, or follows an interest, or socialises (even a little) more, he has an opportunity to meet more people thus increasing his chance of finding a relationship partner. While Mark was sitting at home, not communicating with others, it is incredibly difficult for him to attract a partner. A potential lady will not walk out of the TV screen! (We know it would be good if that could happen, but technology isn't quite there yet!)

In Chrissie's example, she can definitely find happiness in a long-lasting, monogamous intimate relationship with a wonderful worthy man. She just has to believe that. She needs to uncover and identify the negative beliefs that are driving her into the arms of these unavailable, unsuitable men. When she lets go of her old beliefs about herself, and replaces it with a new truth that celebrates her full worth, she will never be anywhere near a man who wasn't her equal.

WHY ARE WE SO UPTIGHT ABOUT DATING?

Last year, while on holiday, Stacey decided to book herself on a day trip on a charter boat which had a mixture of people who wished to go fishing and those who wanted a snorkelling experience off an island nearby.

It was a mixed group, nice people of all ages, and amongst these was a group of men with their families. They had all the fishing gear and fishing gadgets and these guys looked very serious about their sport. So serious, that you couldn't help but feel the tension between them and see the contrast between them and their happy-go-lucky families.

At first, the partners and kids tried to engage the fishermen in conversation by pointing out the beauty around them (turquoise sea, impossibly blue sky, turtles!), but the fishermen brushed them off, wanting to concentrate only on their lures and baits.

As the group left the lagoon, there was a pod of dolphins that joyfully joined them at the bow of the craft and leaped out of the water. Everyone was so excited to see this, squeals of delight from the adults and kids … all except the fishermen who thought that they may 'scare away the fish'.

The food began to be served … really good food, and these men took no interest, with some waving away the yummy delights and peering overboard at their lures.

As the trip progressed, some of the men caught fish. Whoops of happiness echoed from these guys as they got a bite and reeled their catch in. The other, fish-less, men seemed to redouble their efforts, sweating and straining even harder. The longer their catch basket remained empty, the more despondent they became.

The boat arrived at the snorkelling spot and needless to say the group had a wonderful few hours playing and discovering the reef – except for the men who remained on board to change lures and baits.

On the way back one wife said to her husband, 'Wow, that was such a beautiful place and the food!' Her husband, with a small fish in his hands, said, 'Mmm, I wouldn't know. I didn't eat anything much.'

We have seen so many people conducting their search for a romantic love like these fishermen. The search becomes only about landing a fish. In fact, a big fish, THE big fish.

They focus so much on landing this particular fish that the whole life trip is not at all enjoyable, not at all stimulating or fun. They don't enjoy the trip.

When others begin to catch their fish, we begin to panic or get competitive or our vision narrows. After searching long and hard enough, we begin to feel our lures don't work and there must be something wrong with us.

We don't participate in life. We don't see how delicious our life is (the turquoise sea, the impossibly blue sky, the turtles!). We feel lonely and desperate. Life seems dull and half-lived. All because we haven't hooked our Soul Mate.

So, is it any wonder that dating, the process of 'catching The One', makes our palms sweat?

We hear about the stress and pressure associated with 'getting out there' so often from our clients. Some psychologists have attempted to give this dating anxiety a name, but, frankly, it's just stress bought on by fear.

Fear of missing out, fear of being alone, fear of not being good enough, fear of being hurt again, fear of failure, fear of … we could go on, but you know what we are saying by now.

Fear blocks flow. Creative flow, energy flow, the flow of love. We will say this a number of times in this book because this is an important indication of how successful you will be in finding a soul mate quickly and easily.

The exact opposite of fear is joy.

Feel joyful, feel happy, feel appreciative … even feel a bit better than you do now … you block fear and you get moving.

Moving towards freedom, flow and attracting your partner.

SETTING YOURSELF FREE – WHAT HAPPENS WHEN WE CAN'T MOVE ON?

Tissues, Chocolates and Soppy Movies …

As you lie curled up on your bed, eating your hundredth chocolate, mopping up your tears with yet another tissue, watching 'Bridget Jones

Diary' for the fiftieth time, at some stage, you stop and think: 'Hmmm …
I should really get up … or do I actually have to? Maybe I can live in
my pyjamas and really I don't ever have to eat anything but chocolate
again. Life, except for said chocolate, sucks.'

Many of us have felt the pain of experiences like this. We have been
through heartbreak and relationship turmoil. This may have been
because of a relationship break-up or because of one that's pending.
Perhaps it's that terrible, nagging feeling that you may need to end a
relationship but don't know how.

Just as people can be stuck in their past life beliefs, they can also get
stuck within their current lives as well. A very bad break-up may cause
many people to feel as if they simply can't move on to a better place in
their lives or certainly another relationship, with trust and ease.

There is always soul searching that goes on when we end a relationship
or when we have one ended on us.

Some examples of these questions are:

How could he/she do that to me, I love them?

What did I do wrong?

Did they ever love me?

Why did it end, it could have been so special?

Will he/she take me back?

Why do I feel sooooo bad?

I'm sure He/She was my Soul Mate, so why didn't it last forever?

And finally …

How can I stop this from ever happening again?

This is a good thing, this self-reflection and grieving, as it helps
us recognise patterns we may need to address. However, this self
examination should inspire wisdom and action, not lethargy and self-
loathing. Sometimes, in our pain, we get mired in the relationship mud.

Whilst grieving is an important part of any break up, and even wallowing in it for a while is OK, there are some love songs or movies which can, in some way, make us feel that it is fine to be stuck in pain over our relationship woes. Look at the song 'I can't Live without You' by Harry Nilson. This song and others like it are pretty much saying that you have no chance at a happy life if your relationship breaks up. This drives us crazy!

There is so much out there in the media and our culture that says that you should be in a relationship and if you are not, there is something either wrong with you or you are to be pitied. In fact, we have a lot of feedback from people telling us that they feel they can be made to feel left out or socially rejected for not having a partner.

As we spoke about earlier, our belief systems are put into place when we are very young. Sometimes we feel as if we can't move on because of these early belief systems. If we have never been taught at a young age to form healthy bonds and to release in a healthy manner, this of course affects the way we deal with our adult relationships, particularly the beginning and end of one.

So for some of us as adults, we have never learnt how to bond and release well in our relationships. We may hold onto relationships for too long because we are fearful of releasing people. We may wait in hope that we will find nurturing and happiness with someone, even when that person is in no way capable of nurturing us or wanting to. We fall in love with their potential rather than their 'actual'.

That's why it's so important that we learn to nurture ourselves by moving on if this is the healthiest option for us. We have to learn to release people so that we can move on from relationships which are not in our best interests. Once we do this we can make way for a relationship which will work for us.

There are many different reasons why people believe they can't move on after a relationship breaks up. Some examples are:

- Fear. Fear of the unknown, Fear of the known, Fear of abandonment pain. Fear of change. Fear of getting out of their comfort zone … again.
- They are still trying to remain friends. (This is often not real: they want friendship in the hope that it develops back into a relationship)
- They feel that no one else would ever suit them as well
- No one else would want to be in a relationship with them
- They aren't confident about getting back into the dating scene, it feels too scary
- Their ex has moved onto another relationship before they have and they feel revengeful
- They keep comparing everyone else they meet to their ex
- They don't feel like they could ever feel the same way about another person as they do/did about their ex
- They ended the relationship and don't know if their ex would ever take them back
- A 'what if' feeling ('what if' they change, what if the big problem goes away)

If you are still within a relationship that is basically an unhappy one but you can't or won't leave, here are some of the most common reasons why you stay and refuse to move on:

- You feel that you should just settle for what you have – at least, I have a partner and 'I won't feel lonely'
- The partner is extremely controlling and there are safety issues
- You don't want to lose financial security or your home
- You don't want to be blamed for the relationship break-up

- You don't want to hurt family or children by leaving the relationship
- You are fearful of failure and what people will think
- Cultural beliefs
- Society tells you that it is a better and more powerful position to be in if you are partnered (particularly married)
- Guilt
- Fear of change
- You know that it will hurt

Looking at all of these, most of them have fear at the root of the belief.

WHY TIMING IS SO IMPORTANT

Often people become so used to a situation that they truly believe there is nothing they can do to fix or change it. They may stay in a relationship for far too long because it feels as if it's out of their hands, that they can't create what they want in their life or that it's just better to not rock the boat any more. They are AFRAID and feel that the fear is too much for them.

This is NOT true! We CAN create and attract what we want in our lives.

In our practice we often hear our clients describing this as either a 'rut' or that nothing is going 'right'. In spiritual terms we would describe it as a situation of stagnancy, which simply means you have stopped growing.

There is no time like the present to start creating the life you want to live. Fear blocks flow. It does this both mentally and physically, let alone spiritually. Acknowledging the fears by knowing what they are, and deciding that enough is enough and having the courage to move, is the key.

What we have learnt about timing is that the more quickly you move on, the more quickly you can attract the right partner or relationship for you. By making space you invite what you want in. By feeling better, less fearful, by living with a more positive and flow-filled existence.

We would like to offer a few suggestions to assist you to move on more quickly from a relationship break-up. There are a few handy tips that can help speed up the healing process; they are as follows:

- Make a number of dates with yourself and re-discover what your passions are. This may seem hard at first but it pays off extremely quickly
- Go out with friends or family members, don't mope around your home
- Get a new hair cut or some new clothes, something which makes you feel alive and new
- Put away all of the photos, presents and belongings of the ex that you have around your home
- When you feel yourself remembering the good times with the ex, try to write a list of the negative experiences, habits or things that drove you nuts about your ex. This brings the cold hard light of reality into your fantasised view of what life is/was like with them
- Move the furniture around in your home, especially your bedroom. In fact, buy new bed sheets
- Exercise: it boosts the feel-good chemicals in your brain.

All of the things above can be very helpful, but there is another very important thing to do that will help you to move on: it is something ancient and very effective.

THE SOUL DETOX – CUTTING THE CORDS

The idea of body detoxes has become very fashionable these days. There's a liver detox, a kidney detox, a blood detox ... you name the body part, and you can detox it.

We would like to offer you another kind of detox, one that will remove the current relationship toxins. If you like, think of it as a kind of Soul Detox. It's the Cutting of the Cords.

When we show people how to soul detox by Cutting the Cords, even in a large group situation, the feedback we get is very powerful. There is often an instant effect of release and relief. You can cut the cords from anything that you want to release in your life including past and current negative relationships. You can also cut the cord on negative beliefs, patterns and unhelpful self-talk. In this way Cutting the Cord is probably one of the most effective weapons in your obstacle-busting arsenal.

But that doesn't mean that the ritual is a negative one, simply a profound one. It is about removing what is not working for you.

If you are Cutting the Cords purely with your own negative beliefs or behaviours, it means that only these aspects of your personality and life will be removed and not the parts that are authentically useful and desired. There are no drawbacks to this technique.

This process creates change that is far reaching and highly beneficial, however it normally has attached to it emotional processes such as grief, which, normally, is not considered a pleasant or desired state. States such as this, however, are a natural and necessary part of healing and moving on to a life position that is a better one than before. It is a natural part of your own growth as a human being.

If you really are emotional and you don't trust your strength to do this process alone we suggest you do this in consultation with someone you trust who is happy to help you or professionals like ourselves who can facilitate this journey.

If you are getting a friend to assist you we would also encourage the person with you to ensure that they do a simple ritual of grounding and protection prior to beginning the cord-cutting ritual so that they can be a true anchor and guide without getting involved in what is, in fact, a highly emotional experience. These rituals could include simply asking for protection from The Universe or putting themselves in a resourceful state by thinking of something pleasurable or positive.

Exercise: Cutting the Cords

Before starting you need to be very clear that you wish to cut the cords fully with someone or something. If you are removing the negative aspects of a past relationship or even the negative aspects of a current one, Cutting the Cords must be undertaken only when you are ready to move on to a different kind of relationship, as this profound ritual is not easy to reverse.

Take your time with this decision. Cutting the Cords does not necessarily mean you will never have a relationship with this person ever again, it means that you will not have the same kind of relationship with them. It will transform into something that serves you better. If it is better for you to have no relationship with them at all then this will be the outcome.

Gather:

1. Red or Black Candle
2. Sharp knife or scissors for cutting the cord.
3. Cord long enough to go around your waist with enough room to fit your fist between your waist and the cord. Choose the kind of cord that most feels right for you. I favour silver or gold cords but any kind of string or ribbon will do.
4. Tongs or tissues for picking up the cord after it is cut.
5. Small spade for burying the cord.

And of course your support person, if need be, can facilitate you through the ritual.

Timing: We like either dark moon or a waning moon phase to cut cords but it's better you cut them when you feel you should, rather than wait for special moon timing.

Opening, Purpose and Intention

Light your candle with intent by saying: 'Universe, I wish to cut the cords with XX (insert person's name or your own negative beliefs) and wish to do this with protection and love. I wish to move on with my life.' Or 'I am here before you tonight to cut the cords of the belief of xxxxx. I wish to transform the relationship I have with them into something that serves me. I ask for your help and protection tonight.'

Now lie down or kneel down.

Relax. Breathe in the power of The Universe.

Close your eyes and begin to imagine yourself floating in darkness. It's very quiet. It's very beautiful. You are not afraid, nor are you alone completely, as the Universe is there with you. Look around yourself; it is completely and utterly dark.

You can see yourself. It is like you are floating around yourself. You can see all aspects of yourself. Your feet, your back, the top of your head.

Now, travel back inside your own body looking out through your own eyes.

Look around you. The darkness is not so dark any more. There now appear many points of light. Almost like stars. Move closer towards them and you realise that these light points are not stars but people, souls. As you move closer you realise that they are people you know. Past and present. If you are cutting the cords with a belief or pattern imagine a symbol of that pattern or belief as well as people.

You notice that everyone is connected with cords that at first look like spider webs. As you can see you are connected with people too. This is a good feeling as you can see that you are never alone and always supported.

Search now for the person/beliefs that you wish to cut the cords with. When you find them, open your eyes in real life and tie your cord around your waist, leaving it loose, so that it is not big enough to step out of, but big enough at least to put your fist under. Leave room enough that you can cut it or burn it easily and safely.

Sit upright or better still stand up firmly – this is a time for action.

Pick up your knife or scissors, holding them safely pointed down beside you.

Think about, in sensual detail (touch, taste, vision, aural, feeling) your interactions with the person/beliefs you wish to sever. Do not dwell on the good or romantic bits if these are what come to mind first. Be slightly detached around these as if we are still feeling pain in these areas. It is very easy to romanticise or enlarge these as 'bigger' experiences than those that are more unpleasant. Similarly, if you are only thinking of the 'bad' experiences, become slightly detached.

When you believe you are feeling what it is to be connected to this person with all your senses, close your eyes and imagine them in front of you. Look at them ... all of them, not just their eyes, or face. See them in 3D, take in all of them.

Now ensure you see that there are fine cords linking you to them ... they can be as they are so do not edit how they look. Sometimes they appear like fine spider webs, sometimes like thick cords, sometimes plaited and perfect, sometimes rough or fleshy. Notice this, and look at the detail and importantly notice where you are joined on your bodies and how.

You may feel sensations at the location of these. If you are afraid or worried here, ask for your facilitator's help or for The Universe to help you.

Now in your mind's eye, but not in real life, take your sacred knife or scissors and cut through the cord that is linking you to that person or belief, in this way severing the cords that bind you. Say out loud, 'I now cut the cords with you. I release you with love.'

This does not mean that you will not see the person, or feel any other positive emotion towards them. It just means that the nature of the relationship you have now with them will be severed. It will end, or transform into something new.

Thank them for the lessons that they offered and taught you. It is now time to let this relationship with this person or belief, in its current form, go.

Now open your eyes, hold the cord in one hand, and your cutting implement in the other.

State plainly and strongly,

'I cut the cords with XXXX. I want the old connection that does not serve me to be cut away, and for me to be free and renewed.'

Now again recall the person and the relationship in its detail. When you are ready, CUT THE CORDS around your waist. Say, **'I cut the cords that bind me! I let you go with love and honour!'**

Breathe deeply, feel the cords drop from your body (in real life and in the metaphysical world).

Close your eyes and watch as those cords that connected you earlier have fallen or do fall away. If there are any left, cut them in your mind or ask that The Universe assists you with the cutting. Take your time with this. Ensure you cut them all away.

Watch as the person that you have cut the cords with recedes back into the myriad other soul stars. Feel how much lighter you are, feel the difference. Float there for a while enjoying the weightlessness.

When you are ready, begin to bring your awareness back into your room.

Now breathe again deeply and relax.

Open your eyes. All is new and will be better.

Be supported if necessary. Allow yourself to feel what you feel and express this.

Give thanks to The Universe.

Now take special care here in GROUNDING YOURSELF. Take a sip of wine or water and debrief your experience by writing it out or with your Facilitator. Then ensure you completely ground by changing your physical state by dancing, eating a big meal, having a bath. Try not to sleep straight away, even if you feel tired.

Now take special care to destroy or bury the cords. Pick them up with your tongs and try not to touch them with your bare hands. Place the cords in a rubbish bin outside your home or dig a hole in the garden and bury them.

What happens now ...

This is the time to surrender to any messages you have been given or any realisations that may come forward. Ensure that you allow yourself plenty of time to express any further emotions after this ritual – whether they be joy, anger, grief or relief. Be very present in your body and if it's sore or stiff, seek massage or other body work to relieve it.

Things will be very different with the person that you have Cut the Cords with. If you have cut the cords with a belief or patterns, you yourself will feel altered and calmer. How this shows up varies.

We believe that people realise on some level that things have changed after the cords have been severed, and sometimes the person who you have separated from doesn't like it one bit. You have taken your power back and this is not the optimum situation for them. This normally manifests by them contacting you or trying to strengthen the connection whether it's with positive or negative intent.

Take Angelique's example:

'Joe and I had a short relationship and it didn't work out, but we kept sleeping together. I wanted more, hoped for more and accordingly,

I jumped whenever he called. All I would get is sex and then more disappointment. I realised this is not what I wanted, but felt so seduced by his pull on me that I decided to cut the cords with this relationship as it was. As soon as I finished the ritual, literally within minutes, Joe rang me wanting me to go out with him for a 'big one'. Normally, I would jump at the chance but you know what? I had absolutely no compulsion to go! I said 'no' in a really nice way, and he seemed really shocked! I haven't felt the need to hang out with him in a romantic sense since. Best thing is that I have started attracting a few new guys. Amazing.'

Joe 'got' that his hold on Angelique had changed and he called her to pull her back in, to re-establish the cords of control. However, once the current connection is cut things would not be the same again.

Dina divorced her controlling husband and decided to cut the cords so she could move on and her story illustrates the power of this severing:

'Even though we are divorced, we have two children so I had to continue to deal with him and still he kept trying to control me. He would withhold child support, be late on picking the kids up, would speak about me to them in negative ways and all this really scared me. I was very ready to sever our old relationship.

I Cut the Cords. It was an emotional experience and I felt very empowered. It felt like a weight had been lifted.

A few days later he came over to pick up the kids and he was even angrier than usual. He really went for it! He accused me of having an affair, of hiding money … lots of other things. I watched him go crazy and at that moment, I realised that none of it mattered. This was just a reaction. *He* was scared! Things *had* changed.

I didn't react my usual way. I didn't argue or scuttle away. I told him calmly that things have changed and that as we were divorced I could do what I wanted. Things just didn't escalate. After that day I'm not sure whether I changed or he did or both, but not only has he backed off, but I am now open to attracting another relationship. I never thought I would even consider this!'

Anton chose to Cut the Cords with beliefs that did not serve him, with rewarding results:

'I felt that I had dealt with my old relationships pretty well but I had some beliefs that I wanted to get rid of. I identified that my workaholism was standing in the way to attracting and keeping a partner. My last three girlfriends, who I had met at work, had complained that I worked too hard, didn't focus at all on them, and that my Blackberry got more action than they did … and you know, unfortunately they were right.

So I cut the cords with my need to work so obsessively and this decision was harder than I thought. I worried that I would lose my job, my status, my edge, even my buddies. What tipped the scales for me was this vision of being alone with just my laptop for company. Having a partner and a balanced life seemed worth the risk.

I got to work the next day and my boss tells me that I would be required to work the weekend. Normally I would just automatically say OK, but this time something inside me said 'no'. It just popped out!

I questioned why he asked me and he said, 'Mate, it's just that you always say yes and I didn't need to ask anyone else. You never seem to mind. But it's no problem, I can ask someone else.'

I realised that I was the only one he ever asked simply because I was always willing.

Whilst I still work long hours I am certainly actively seeking balance now. What's more (3 months later) I have attracted a woman that I think is a keeper. I met her *outside* work. There is no way she would be with me now if I couldn't spend time with her.'

Cutting the Cords with a relationship or patterns and beliefs that do not serve you enable you to clear the slate and start afresh with no obstacles in the way. It releases old fears and rejuvenates the real you. It gives you the energy, passion and focus to relax about deciding what you really want in your life now and allows you a clear channel to attract it in.

So what are you waiting for?

SECTION 3

ATTRACTING YOUR IDEAL PARTNER

HOW THE LAWS OF ATTRACTION WORK WITH LOVE

There has been a lot of publicity and general hoo-ha about the concept of the Law of Attraction over the past few years. Whilst the ancient law, common to many cultures and spiritual traditions, is incredibly useful, there is so much confusion about what it is and how it works.

We would need a whole book to describe the Law of Attraction as it applies to Love (and there are a myriad of books like this out there) but again, we want to get to the nitty gritty; we want to simplify things so you understand what you need to know *right now*, to get results.

Put simply, the Law of Attraction is concerned about emotional energy, vibration and choice. For those of you who intellectually struggle with this idea of vibration and energy, think of this process as a choice about emotional attitude.

Everything is made up of energy. Every kind of energy vibrates at its own frequency or vibrational level. It is believed that when we are a direct vibrational match to what we are asking for, it flows into our lives. This is the Law of Attraction.

So in short, Like Attracts Like. If you want something, the easiest and fastest way to get it is to become its vibrational match. To do that, we need to be very clear about what we want and to be aware of how we feel about it. The more positive we feel, the more we attract something positive. The more negative we feel (and this includes fear, anger, doubt and hopelessness) the further away we push it.

This law is particularly potent when it comes to Soul Mates.

With the attraction of a Romantic Soul Mate, we presume you want someone ideal for you. Someone better than you have experienced before. However, if you are giving off a confused set of emotions and vibes, what you will tend to attract is what you are giving off … and that's not what you are really after. If you keep doing this what you get is negative patterns that keep you in an unhealthy, unhappy situation, even though you don't want to be there. We will talk about these patterns later in this section.

Where this all starts is with you. You need to be living, thinking and feeling as positively as you can. *As you can* is the important aspect here: no one is asking you to be joyful and happy all the time – there are going to be times of stress or unhappiness or frustration. If someone hurts you it is not appropriate to be unrealistically happy about it. That is not emotionally intelligent.

What the Law of Attraction asks you to do is move to an emotion that feels a bit better. Any emotion! And then you move to a better one and again to a better one and then you do this consciously until you are indeed experiencing an emotion that is a pleasurable one for you. That's all.

Witches speak of this as being 'pleasure-led'. A really easy way to keep this positive energy or attitude in your life is to make decisions based on whether or not it will be pleasurable for you. Pleasure is a 'feel good' emotion and some of you may have a strong reaction to

this. 'That sounds selfish!' we have heard people say. 'I have a duty to look after others.'

We are not telling you that you take every day off work because you would prefer to go shopping or sailing instead. But we are saying that you should go shopping or sailing or whatever else it is that makes you very happy at a more appropriate time if that is what gives you pleasure, not just work. We are not saying that you shouldn't fulfill your obligations, but if all your obligations are a burden, if there is very little room in your life for your own pleasure, we would question the quality of your life. We would then question what it is that you could or would attract.

We will only attract what we are. Like will attract like. So if we want to attract positive things we need to be giving out positive vibrations.

By deeply engaging in life, by choosing to experience emotions that make us feel positive and by having a positive vision for ourselves, this prepares a fertile and welcoming place for another person to be attracted into.

What would you most like to attract to you … a happy person living a great balanced life or a volatile person living an unhappy, unbalanced life?

We are presuming you would prefer the first example … but you can't be like the second person and want the first. Even if we are lucky enough to attract the first and we are more like the second, it may not last long!

WHY HAVING A GREAT LIFE IS THE BEST WAY TO CREATE A GREAT LOVE

'I'm so miserable. My heart has been broken for so long I don't know what I want to do any more,' said Fiona, a 35-year-old graphic designer from Sydney.

Fiona had broken up with Mike, her partner of three years, over 12 months earlier and had come for a consult to work out a strategy to reduce her pain and to move forward.

Stacey asked her to describe her current life and just why she felt so awful.

'Mike and I had a great life in that it was full of things that we did as a couple. We travelled together, cooked together, played together and set up house. I was part of a couple, which I loved. And then, when it ended, I had nothing! I don't really do anything half as fun as what I did with him. It's like I am empty. '

Feeling empty is a very apt description of what many people, in particular women, experience after a break-up. Unfortunately, this is because they have often negated their own needs in favour of the other person's or the relationship's needs. Our authenticity suffers (and the relationship) if we can't keep our own pleasures and independence.

Remember like attracts like. The vibe we give out is the vibe we attract. The more Fiona concentrates on the perceived emptiness of her life, the less flow she gets towards her intention and her life stays 'empty'.

Stacey set Fiona some homework. She advised Fiona to concentrate on building her own internal power levels first by exercising her right to pleasure. (Sounds like awful homework, doesn't it?)

'Fiona, tell me what it is that you just love doing. Perhaps it's something you did before you met Mike?' Stacey enquired.

Fiona thought for a while and began to cry and said, 'This is so awful. I have forgotten what it is that makes me happy. I just do what I have to do. How disgusting. I get what you are saying now. I have forgotten myself. How could I have let myself go for so long?'

Fiona related how she used to surf but hadn't really since she partnered with Mike. She also explained that she used to go away each month on weekends away with her girlfriends. These trips were manna for the mind and body and she realised how much of a difference they made to her stress levels and her levels of drive.

'We used to go away as a group and it was always girlie and very nourishing. We would check in on where our lives were headed but it was just a really fun shot in the arm! We would talk out our problems, connect and no matter what was going on things would be better once that weekend was over.'

So we agreed that Fiona would take up surfing again and restart the weekends as a way to raise her energy levels. She would also consciously choose things that would give her pleasure over the boring 'coulds' and 'shoulds' in her life. She would make her decisions from a place of 'what feels best' rather than duty. This would bring her vibrations to a more positive level and therefore allow this to match a more attractive energy.

Three weeks later Fiona emailed. 'I cannot tell you how much better I feel! I have just come back from our first weekend away and I cried with gratitude at the end of it! As for the surfing … I'm rusty but I so love it. I don't think about anything except for getting on that wave and that is so freeing. I have also thought of a couple of other things I want to do now, like joining the surf club and maybe going back to Uni to do my PhD.'

A month later Fiona came in to the office, ready for the next step. 'Hey, this pleasure homework – it's the best homework I have ever done. You know, three weeks ago I just wanted to feel a bit better but now I am ready for someone new! And call me crazy, but I know there are two guys I have known for a while giving me the eye at the café near the beach and this was soooo not happening before!'

So what was it that made those two guys take notice of her? Is it just her noticing them at last? Them noticing her just now? Perhaps. More likely it's that she is enjoying life. More likely that she is giving off a new positive energy and her vibes are different! They are much more a match to other people who are enjoying their lives in a more balanced way.

When we break up with someone it is right to feel grief. This is healthy and normal. It is also a time to reclaim who we are.

It is an opportunity to move forward through the grief and pain and begin another time of our lives, wiser and better. If we stay stuck and stagnant in this grief or stagnant energy for too long, we cease to grow and move. This makes attracting anything or anyone positive very difficult.

Similarly, if we want to improve an existing relationship, the place to start is with our *own* energy. Remember: Like attracts like. We cannot change others but we can change our selves. This change, this positive change, triggers a change in others … but it definitely starts with us.

This is a personal responsibility that puts the power back in our hands. We can control what we want to be experiencing. We can control who we attract.

If we are enjoying life, putting out more positive energy, more positive vibes, then the law of attraction cannot help but respond in kind. You will attract more positive people and if it be your desire, a partner that is more suitable and positive for you far faster than if you choose to have a more negative outlook.

A participant at our workshops once said to us, 'So what you want me to do is have such a great life that the man ends up being the cherry on the cake, not the whole yummy cake. You want me to have such a great life that when he does come, it's no big surprise or no big deal.'

Exactly!

We want you to not worry about whether or not he/she will come. If you have doubt, well, that's not a great vibe. If you have feared that he/she will not come into your life, even though you are asking for it, that gives The Universe a mixed message, which just slows things down.

We want you to be so very happy and so very clear that there is no room for doubt, no room for fear and no room to feel pain that they are not in your life yet. This gives out such a powerful and clean magnetic pull that the Universe just simply co-creates this with you. And suddenly, yet expectantly, there they are!

Having a great life combined with a clear intention is indeed the best way to attract a great love!

But what kind of person is right for you?

ASKING FOR EXACTLY WHAT YOU WANT

When we do our 'Soul Mates with No Excuses' workshops, we ask the question 'Does everyone know what they want?'

And the response is always a resounding 'yes!'.

So, true to form, we test the group, by calling forward a couple of the most enthusiastic nodders.

We enquire: 'So tell me exactly the kind of relationship that you want in one short sentence.'

The person looks very puzzled for a second. Actually we would call it a 'tharn'; which is the name of the 'paralysed in the headlights trance' that rabbits get as described in the book '*Watership Down.*'

They then come out with one of two things: either a very lengthy description of the kind of person they want, or a list of the things they don't want.

For example: 'Oh, I want a man who is kind and treats me well, I want to get married and he would be a good father and he is fun to be with and … and … and … and …'

Or

'I want someone who won't cheat on me, someone who is not a slacker, someone who isn't going to disrespect me or not like my family, someone who …'

But at this point, we have only asked them a single simple question '… Exactly what *kind* of relationship do you want?' We have also requested they do it in one simple sentence.

The first step in finding a partner, one that is ideal for you right now, is to know clearly and concisely the nature of the relationship that you seek.

This is an intensely personal decision. What is right for you may not be right for someone else. What you decide right now may also change, and this is totally fine, but right now, this minute, you need to know beyond any reasonable doubt the kind of relationship you wish to be experiencing.

Without having this clarity, you cannot attract it.

So what are some options?

- Do you want a long term committed relationship leading to marriage?
- Do you want a shorter term committed relationship?
- Do you want a friend with benefits?
- Do you want a companion to have fun with but no sexual ties?
- Do you want a series of dates that are nothing too serious but loads of fun?

The list is almost endless.

So, decide what you want, and ensure that it is in positive language. This means no 'I don't wants' or 'nots'. For example, if you wanted a long term committed relationship, simply ask for that, not a 'long term relationship where the guy doesn't cheat'.

NOW TO THE NEXT STEP …

We then ask the workshop group, who by then are a little savvier to the process,

'Who knows the attributes of the person they wish to attract?'

This time we have lots more waving hands in the air. We ask two or three to tell us. Almost all of the participants we call up can only give us six or seven attributes before they come out with 'Yep, that's pretty much it'. It's worth noting here that we always give them unlimited time and they are happy to share.

Six or seven attributes are not enough. Not nearly enough. Choosing any kind of love partner is one of the biggest and most important decisions of your life, yet, most people can only describe less than a double handful of attributes before they run out of steam. Most women would do better describing the next pair of shoes they wish to buy.

We insist on a minimum of thirty descriptive attributes in our workshops. Yes, *thirty*. Let us reassure you that most participants, by the time we have 'finished with them', have far more than that and find the process interesting and fun.

What you are going to do is write down your list of attributes. All the attributes you describe should be in the positive – what you *do* want rather than what you *don't*. The only time we may think of what we don't want is a tool to help us decide what we would now prefer. A great way to flush out what you want in a partner is to think about what we don't want and 'flip it'.

We think that people are naturally able to state what they don't want more articulately than what they do, particularly if they have been burnt in previous relationships.

For example:

You may think: I don't want someone who will cheat on me.

Flip it to: I want someone who is faithful and committed.

You may think: I don't want someone who is neurotic and angry.

Flip it to: I want someone who is emotionally intelligent.

Get it?

Of course, you can also think back on the positive aspects of past relationships for inspiration, but do not dwell on the person, just the attribute.

The other key aspect of creating this list is asking for the things that may challenge you, things that will heal the patterns that you have had previously.

One of the first things Stacey added to her attribute list when wishing to finally attract a husband was that she could have an equal partner. This actually meant that she would have to change too if she was to break her pattern. Remember, it all starts with you.

So make your list and spend some decent time on it. Allow the idea to mull over in your mind and as you sleep. Get excited about it … after all, you are planning your romantic future.

Mia's List for an Ideal Partner

Mia is an attractive, bright 31-year-old lawyer who kindly allowed us to share her list here as a working example.

Mia wanted to meet someone brilliant and get married. She has experienced a string of 2-year-long relationships that have ended by her partner cheating on her. This made her more suspicious of the 'next' man and she became unnecessarily needy and insecure, setting up a kind of vicious cycle which led to distrust and volatility which led to the cheating. Mia wanted not only to attract a great guy but also to learn to trust again.

This is Mia's list …

Kind of Relationship:
I want a long term, committed relationship leading to marriage.

My ideal partner:

- Is loving
- Is faithful (DB)
- Is trustworthy (DB)
- Is open-minded (DB)
- Is funny
- Is creative
- Is intelligent
- Is enthusiastic about life
- Likes to travel
- Likes animals
- Is open to having children
- Is geographically close

- Is very sexy and very attractive!
- Is a good lover
- Is outdoors orientated
- Is fit
- Is a good communicator
- Is honest
- Likes to learn
- Is handy around the home
- Can cook
- Is expressive
- Likes a wide variety of music
- Gets on well with my family
- Is ambitious
- Is financially secure or on the way to being financially secure
- Is independent
- Is balanced between work and home
- Cares about others actively
- Is emotionally intelligent

It's a great list, isn't it? You can almost picture the type of person that this is.

Mia has done a brave thing too. She has asked for a faithful and trustworthy partner as well as someone very attractive. This indicates her willingness to have faith that she can attract someone who will not let her down this time. Even more importantly, this also signals her willingness to trust that she will be able to 'step-up' into a relationship with a man who is 'perfect' for her.

DEAL BREAKERS

When we look at our Ideal Partner list, at first glance every attribute looks as important as the other. There are, however, some attributes that are so important that without them we just could not entertain having a love relationship with a person for any length of time.

We like to call these elements **Deal Breakers**.

Deal Breakers are just what the term sounds like: they are non-negotiable desires which are vital for the commencement and/or continuance of the relationship.

On Mia's list, she listed faithful and open minded as deal breakers (DB).

Mia explains:

'I have had boyfriends in the past who have been playing around on me when we had agreed on an exclusive relationship. When this happened, I broke up the relationship straight away. Being unfaithful is certainly something I see as a deal breaker.

'At the same time, I am very open-minded in nature. I like to discover new things and I have a real love of difference: cultural, physical, spiritual, a live-and-let-live attitude. People that are really controlling or extreme have no place in my life. To go out with someone who was racist or had really fundamentalist religious views would be impossible for me.'

Every person is unique and naturally will have different views on what a deal breaker may be for them. Whilst many of us may agree with Mia that faithfulness is a key part of a long term committed relationship, other people certainly do not. Also if you were not asking for a long term committed relationship and instead perhaps asking for a shorter term 'getting over the hump' relationship, having exclusivity is not the emphasis.

There are no excuses for being ignorant about what your personal deal breakers are. Knowing yourself more deeply and knowing what you will and will not bear saves you a hell of a lot of drama and heartache down the track. I cannot tell you the amount of women and men we have consulted with who either were ignorant of their deal breakers or, worse, knew them yet still decided to try and change the other person to fit their ideal.

If you ignore your deal breakers you may not just pick the wrong person (disaster!), we can almost guarantee that you'll never have the happy, peaceful relationship that you seek.

NEGOTIABLES

Whilst there are always deal breakers on our lists there are always more elements that are less finite for us. With these elements there is room to move and negotiate between you.

We call these elements **Negotiables**.

Negotiables are still preferred attributes but there is room to negotiate between the partners.

If you are resourceful and both you and your partner are capable of compromise, we doubt that you would decide to leave a partner because of a negotiable.

For example, on Mia's list she has listed 'geographically close' and 'handy around the home' as negotiables.

She comments:

'I don't like the idea of having a long-distance relationship because I think that they must be really hard work but if I met someone amazing who happened to live a distance away from me, I think I have the maturity to give it a good shot.

'Similarly having a guy who is handy around the house would be perfect … as I am not so good with a hammer or electrics … but would it stop me from having a relationship if everything else was pretty good? Nope!'

We would particularly agree with these two choices as negotiables. Stacey is very happily married to a man she had a long distance relationship with in the first year and she has her own tool box.

Negotiables free you from being too picky about what you want and allow you to get very clear about what is truly important to you.

GETTING PRACTICAL

Look at your list and begin to think about what are absolute Deal breakers for you and what are Negotiables.

Mark the Deal breakers in red or put a red star or DB next to the attribute.

Negotiables can be marked in green or with an N placed beside them.

Doing this truthfully may take some time and a bit of soul-searching, but the results are worth it. What this will give you is an accurate guide to what is honestly important to you now … a list of your desires when it comes to an ideal partner.

There are two wonderful things we can do with this information now. Firstly, we can have it on hand to match the people we attract from now on. This gives us an even clearer description of what we are looking for and forewarns us against what we really don't want. This enables our decision making process to be incredibly clear and simple. A real 'no excuses' approach!

Secondly, we can now put some spiritual power behind our list and send it out to the Universe, ensuring its fulfilment.

Now we are going to share with you an incredibly effective way to attract your ideal partner faster. It's by combining everything that you have learned in this section all in one swoop.

ATTRACTING AN IDEAL PARTNER

You now know that the law of attraction cannot help but respond to a clear, positive, vibrational command and, even if you don't wish to believe in 'this kind of thing', having clarity around and putting active positive energy towards an intention is a proven way to move forward. But let's go back to the spiritual laws …

You have thought about what you want, you have even gone to the trouble of knocking out obstacles ahead of time (particularly doubt) and you now have a list. The next thing the spiritual laws require is to place some energy behind your intention … and not just any kind of energy … positive energy.

The idea of raising and releasing energy towards a purpose is an ancient one and it is at the heart of many spiritual practices, particularly those who use ritual such as witchcraft and shamanism. This energy, this e-motion, is raised by various easy methods and propels the intention, just like a rocket out towards the Universe. It also anchors what we desire securely within our unconscious mind, which of course is the part of the mind that really drives us.

Now, you may be one of those people who would never have entertained the idea of casting a spell. Perhaps even the word 'spell' makes you nervous. If this is so, just substitute the word Technique. It is the same thing; it is just a label.

If you love the idea of casting a spell, or are used to it if you are of the Witchy persuasion, you will love this one! Either way, we have never met a client who doesn't find the process of spell casting (or completing this technique) an enjoyable one.

We know this technique works due to the high success rate and the amount of positive feedback we have had. This is the very same spell that Stacey used to attract her lovely husband and the same spell that our clients below have used …

'I can't believe how quick it was. I met someone in the gym two weeks later after not having anyone for years! He was almost exactly what I asked for, except for one or two minor negotiables.' **Dani, Sydney**.

'I asked specifically for a 'friend with benefits'. I was getting over a really bad break-up and although I wanted some company, I did not want a serious thing yet. And a month later, there he was.' **Bernadette, Perth**.

'I have had some very bad luck with women. I realised that I wasn't really clear about what I wanted and my bad luck was me! I did the list and the spell and Emma came along. It was like a mirage! I thought 'this couldn't be real it was so perfect' but it was.' **Patrick, Bondi**.

'I had never ever thought about doing anything like the spell bit. It was fun but powerful at the same time. I'm not spiritual, so to me it was a bit like self-hypnosis. Didn't really matter what it was, it's what it did. I asked to be dating again, and that's what it generated for me.' **Alissa, London, UK**.

Spell to Attract an Ideal Partner
BEFORE YOU START:

It is worth telling you a few things about these kinds of techniques before you do them. Firstly, they work. You will experience change. And this can sometimes be quick or dramatic. Whilst this may make you feel very happy on first thought, change may not be easy nor may it look wonderful at first. Decide if this is right for you. If it is and change does occur and it feels uncomfortable, surrender. Just stay with it and participate (move) as The Universe responds to your desire. Things will move to a place where you can see your progress in a happier light.

Secondly, when we do spells to attract love we never ever cast on, or for, a particular person. This is very tempting for some people. If we do this, we interfere with free will, a huge 'no-no'.

Sometimes people come to us for a consult in the hope that they can make their ex fall back in love with them or get the guy next door they have been pining for to go out on a date. If we agreed to do this, we would be interfering with their free will. How would you like it if someone cast a spell on you to fall in love with them and you didn't feel that way?

Instead, what we do is a much more ethical yet effective thing. We cast for our ideal attributes (not the person). If this person is indeed the one we describe, well, hey, we have a winner! If not, someone else will step forward and, well, hey, again we have a winner. Win–win.

And finally, the more positive emotion you can put behind your intention the more effectively the technique works. Enjoy yourself! If you are worried about following the instructions carefully read them beforehand, record them on your iPod or you can buy beautifully produced audio copies. The resources section (p.118) at the back of this book has details of suppliers.

Don't worry if the candle or the herbs go out … simply relight them. If you are feeling anxious, change that into anticipation. Don't think (we do enough of that obsessive stuff) … enjoy and play instead.

Now let's go for it.

PREPARATION

Ensure that you will be undisturbed.

Have your intention clearly in mind or written down.

For example:

'My intention tonight is to attract a partner that is ideal for me, quickly and easily.' Or 'I wish to attract a long term committed relationship leading to marriage quickly and easily.'

Before the spell, you would have taken some considerable time out to think about both the kind of relationship you want and the attributes of the ideal partner that you wish to attract.

Please double-check that your language is all positive and again it is very important that you do not cast for someone you know. Once you have your 'attribute list' go over it one more time to be sure and then cast.

Gather:

1. Red or white candle

2. Matches

3. Ceramic Bowl

4. Pen and Paper

5. Herbs

I prefer mugwort, sweet basil, rose petals and 'bats blood' or frankincense for this spell and you only need a pinch of each. The first 3 ingredients can be found in almost any health food shop, and bats blood or frankincense (resins) can be found in magical supply stores or by ordering from Stacey at www.themodernwitch.com. If you can't obtain them all, that's OK … just burn ordinary incense instead.

6. Your list of attributes

7. A piece of jewelery or an object you can use as a talisman (charged item)

It needs to be something you can wear or carry fairly constantly.

FOCUS

Dim the lights and relax. Breathe deeply.

If you know how, cast and open a Circle if you wish, but this is completely optional.

Light the candle, and *state your intent out loud.*

Take several deep breaths. Relax.

BUILDING POWER

Now take your list and begin to read all the attributes OUT LOUD. Do this with emotion … really feel it!

Read through the list again, building your emotion.

Once you have done this twice, close your eyes and begin to imagine spending a day with this ideal partner.

Enjoy this!

What do they sound like? What do they look like? What are you doing together? Take your time doing this.

You should begin to feel very good with positive emotions like excitement, passion; love and joy begin to rise in your Self.

Open your eyes and now read your list out loud again, one last time, this time more strongly.

See this and FEEL this ideal partner clearly in your mind and body. Feel your personal vitality. Feel it warm you, pulse through you.

Breathe in deeply. As you breathe in, imagine you are inhaling even more power from the earth, the trees, the moon, the sky, the Universe. Everything is conspiring FOR you!

Begin to chant:

Come to me! Come to me!
Grow and be real,
Come to Me! Come to me!
Partner Ideal!

Chant faster and faster, and when you feel as though your emotion is at its highest, lean the list close to the flame and set it on fire! (Avoid burning your fingers by placing the burning paper in the bowl.)

This releases your intention to the Universe and the unconscious.

Then light your herbs or incense. Take your talisman and pass it through the smoke.

As you do this, say out loud:

'I charge this talisman with attraction. It will draw my ideal partner to me quickly and easily.'

Relax and breathe deeply.

Know that the Universe has heard your intention and is acting already, flowing people, places and things towards the fulfillment of your intention.

Ask The Universe: **'What do I need to do now to make this happen faster?'**

Allow the answer(s) to come and write them down. (Notice we say 'allow' and not 'think'. Do not think of an answer, listen instead!) You will action these later.

Blow out the candle, with thanks to The Universe.

You have cast the spell! CONGRATULATIONS! Know that your ideal partner is already heeding this energy and is growing towards you. Accept this fact in your own body and relax into this knowingness.

Take the charged talisman and keep it with you constantly.

It's a reminder of your intention and your active participation. Keep it with you and try to let no one else touch it. If it is a piece of jewellery keep it on, if it's something else keep it in your bag, purse or pocket as much as you can.

Write down everything The Universe has instructed you to do on your ACTION PLAN. Yes … an Action Plan … It's on page 97.

Action whatever you have written down. You may also dream of things to action. The key here is to move and co-create.

Chart your progress on your Action Plan by recording your feelings, behaviours, actions and results. This allows you to both ensure you are moving forward and mark your participation, paying close attention to coincidences and details even if they seem insignificant or unrelated at the time.

YOUR ACTION PLAN FOR GUARANTEED RESULTS

We think you would realise by now that we are particularly enamoured by the word 'action'. Getting you to make the first move towards what you want is like watching the first domino fall in a long line towards the last one to fall. You have to push the first one over for the process to begin.

To make this process easier, we have created a Personal Action Plan. This ensures you know what to do next and that you begin to participate.

You will notice it has a space for your signature at the bottom. This is not meant to be a fluffy addition. Taking ownership and responsibility for your journey is crucial to its success. Sign it only if you are committed.

A really good idea is to share this with a good friend who will check on you every now and again to make sure you are doing everything you have promised you would do. This helps knock out any residual traces of self-sabotage.

Again, the key here is to take action. Action leads to results.

You may be tempted to leave out this Action Plan, believing that you are ready to move forward without it. Maybe so! However, our best results have come from people using it and actioning it.

The Universe loves you and wants clear direction in order to satisfy what it is you really want. By completing all the exercises we have set and by taking action on your plan, you will be co-creating in an incredibly powerful way … no excuses!

Soul Mates Action Plan

For_____

_____

Relationship Intention (What kind of relationship do you want right now?)

_____
_____
_____

Attributes of my Ideal Partner: (Including Deal breakers)

_____
_____
_____
_____
_____

My Actions are:

_____
_____
_____
_____
_____

Timeframe:_____

Signed by

SECTION 4

OTHER TOOLS TO ENHANCE THE PROCESS

Candles, Crystals and Talismans

The techniques and insights we have given you in this book should certainly have been helpful and started you well on your way to identifying and attracting a happy, healthy relationship. But there are other tools, techniques and objects which have been used throughout many cultures to enhance the process of attracting an ideal partner. Many of these tools are tried and tested; they produce wonderful results.

In this section we have listed some of our favourite tools to help you to attract or enhance a relationship.

Candles

Candle Magic has been used as a focus point for thousands of years for many different cultures and religions. Whether you are a Christian, Jew or even Native American you would use fire to state your intent. It is like asking the Universe or unconscious mind to pay attention because we are ready to have a chat.

We like to think that you could use this candle magic to enhance all aspects of your life whether you are setting intentions as a single person or as a couple.

The ideal colours of the candles would be red, pink, orange, white or green. However if you don't have any of these coloured candles, don't let that hold you back. Rather than not doing anything at all, you can use any colour candle within your reach.

It's important to use a new candle to place your intent onto. Don't be tempted to use an old emergency candle or one that was used for your Aunt's birthday cake last year.

When you are ready, it's time to set the intention for your candle.

What do you want to attract to you?

What emotion do you need to focus on?

Once you have chosen the emotion or energy that you would like to attract, look down at the chart below and see what the corresponding colour of the candle will be.

Candles

Colour	Symbol	Energy/Emotion to attract
Red	Full Blown Love	Passion Increase Lust Strength
Pink	Gentle Love	Affection Romance Caring
Orange	Warms a cold heart	Creativity Success in Relationship Financial Strength
White	Clear and Remove Negativity	Purity New Beginnings Renewal
Green	Moving Forwards	Growth Fertility Abundance

Exercise: Using Candle Magic to Attract Intention

When you are ready, go into your bedroom, turn down the lights and centre yourself. Make sure that you will not be disturbed.

Relax, get comfortable!

Light your candle, breathe deeply and take time to focus on what you want to bring into your relationship area.

Once you can see what it is that you want to achieve in your mind, visualise yourself happy, fulfilled and loved. Feel the energy surround you and know now that you have put your wish out to the Universe.

You can now relax, believe and know that you are well on your way to manifesting your desired result.

When you have finished, snuff your candle, don't blow it out. Keep your candle in a special place and do not use it for any other purposes. You can repeat this process for three nights in a row if you wish.

<u>Crystals</u>

Crystals are not only used for their healing properties, they are also used in many different common household objects such as quartz crystal in wristwatches. Quartz is piezoelectric which means that it has a very small electric current which runs through it. If you gently hold a quartz crystal in your hand you can feel this current or vibration.

All crystals (not only quartz crystal) have their own vibration. *Using crystals for healing* can help you attract certain things to you, for example love or abundance. Crystals can also strengthen the body and remove energy blockages which may cause disease.

By holding or wearing crystals as a talisman you can attract or enhance your relationship area.

It's very important to cleanse crystals to remove any previously stored energy or negativity. Crystals can be cleansed in any of the following different ways:

- Place crystals in direct sunlight for at least 5 hours (watch out with clear quartz that you don't cause a fire)
- Smudge crystals with incense or a smudge stick
- Bury the crystals in the earth, cover the crystals with dirt and leave for three days
- Spray crystals with a space-clearing spray
- Place crystals on a large piece of Amethyst

Note: We don't recommend using salt water to cleanse crystals as it can damage the crystal and/or remove its natural sheen.

To charge a crystal and give it extra energy, place the crystal out in the moonlight on a full moon.

We recommend the use of the following crystals to enhance your relationship area:

Crystals

Crystal	Symbol	Energy to attract
Rose Quartz	The Stone of Love	Unconditional love Self love Romantic love
Garnet	The Stone of Commitment	Passion Devotion Sexuality
Ruby	The Stone of Nobility	Nurturing Courage Loyalty
Smoky Quartz	The Stone of Co-operation	Release Grounding Balance
Clear Quartz	The Stone of Power	Harmony Clarity Calmness
Peridot	———	Stimulates the Heart Common Sense Balance

Crystal	Symbol	Energy to attract
Aventurine	——	Self Confidence Clarity Creativity
Amethyst	The Stone of Spirituality	Protection Calming Relaxation
Citrine	The Merchant's Stone	Creativity Optimism Self Knowledge
Tiger Eye	——	Warmth Grounding Sexual Discipline

Herbs and Plants

Almost every culture has a substantial herbal history. Plants have been used traditionally for health, culinary purposes, decoration and as spiritual assistants as far back as we can trace. Possibly their most important uses have been to treat illnesses and for magical purposes.

Whilst we have all used herbs to flavour up our favourite dish, many of us have never used herbs to assist us in other areas of our life, including love. Aphrodisiacs are probably the most famous uses of herbs and plants in regard to love. Lust and attraction is said to increase in all manner of ways through the powers of plants. Famous aphrodisiacs include mandrake, belladonna, garlic (yes, garlic!), jasmine and poppy. Whilst the jury may be out on the effectiveness of mandrake and belladonna (they are actually poisons at the wrong dosage) medical science can back up the effects of garlic and ginseng as stimulants and jasmine as a relaxant.

Today, there are laws in most countries ensuring only trained herbalists, naturopaths and medical practitioners can prescribe botanical remedies for internal use. We are not personally medical practitioners, and as such, legally cannot advise you to take any herbs, woods or flower derivatives internally or topically for health reasons. However, we want to introduce herbs to you in regard to the way they can work for you within spiritual rituals and techniques when it comes to love, sex and attraction.

Modern spiritual practitioners use oils, herbs and other plants to help them focus on attraction and empowering themselves and their clients. We believe using plants is a synergistic process: it's their individual energy mixed with our signature energy that does the work very efficiently, yet gently.

Herbs, flowers and oils can be used for all manner of purposes that would be useful for those interested in attracting Soul Mates including:

- To encourage stress relief and relaxation
- To encourage attraction of all kinds
- Opening the psychic channels associated with past lives
- To heal the grief and pain associated with break-ups
- To cut cords
- To promote peace and reconciliation
- As aphrodisiacs

Below is a table of the most effective herbs and plants for the attraction of love, lust and better relationships. Feel free to combine as you wish.

Herbal Consultant Table
Herbs can be obtained through witchcraft supply stores, fresh from most produce shops or, better still, by growing a garden of your own.

WAYS TO USE HERBS
Burning on Charcoal
Small charcoal blocks can be used as a base to burn almost any dried plant to evoke the energies and to add a beautiful scent. This is also a common way to use herbs in spells. Always start with a small amount of one of the resin plants, such as frankincense or myrrh, or one of the woods such as

sandalwood should you want a fragrant base. Then add a pinch or two of the other herbs you have decided on. Then light the charcoal and watch and enjoy as the fragrant smoke rises – as does your intention!

Sprinkled

A very ancient way of changing the energies of an area is to sprinkle the environment with plant energy.

So, if you haven't had a romantic visitor to your bedroom in some time why not change that energy by sprinkling some aphrodisiac or herbs of attraction over your bed such as catnip, jasmine flowers, vervain or saffron. Take a teaspoon of no more than three herbs plus a teaspoon of sea salt and sprinkle. Enjoy!

In Bags

A very ancient way of using herbs for attraction is to place different varieties of chosen herbs in small material bags. These bags can then be carried on your person, in your handbag or even placed in your workplace or bedroom. Simply choose whatever herbs contain the energies that you wish to absorb and place a teaspoon of each in the bag.

Herbs

Name	Wisdom
Acacia	Love, protection, psychic powers
Angelica	Banishes hostility from others, protection, healing, warming
Ash	Expansion of horizons, healing, strength
Azalea	Hidden emotions, exposing secrets
Basil	Love, soul detox, conquers fears of stepping up
Bay Leaf	Protection, healing, purification, strength
Birch	Cleansing, health, wisdom, new beginnings
Borage	Aids the expression of sorrow, working through grief
Cactus	Protection, purity
Calamus	Healing, protection, helps bind long distance lovers

Caraway	Passion, health, wisdom
Catnip	Happiness in the home and every day
Chicory	Invisibility in hostile situations, removing obstacles, receiving favours, melts frigidity both mentally and physically
Chilli	Heats up waning relationships, heats up passion
Cinnamon	Spirituality, success, healing, building of intuition, passion and love
Clover	Luck in love, happiness
Devils Shoestring	Wealth and protection
Dragons Blood	Love, magic, protection, dispels negativity, increase male potency
Eucalyptus	Clarity, strength
Fenugreek	Attraction, seduction
Fig	Wisdom, creativity and creation, fertility, harmony and balance
Frankincense	Increasing self-esteem, intuition, positivity, aphrodisiac
Garlic	Aphrodisiac, protection, healing, banishing negativity, warming and toning
Guinea Pepper	Dispels negativity
Honeysuckle	Protection and relaxation
Jasmine	Lust, seduction, building of feminine power, aphrodisiac
Juniper	Protection against negative forces, love, banishing
Lavender	Love, protection (especially of children), peace
Lemon Balm	Calming, purification
Licorice	Cleansing, attraction
Lotus/Water Lily	Spiritual regeneration, reveals secrets
Mandrake	Aphrodisiac, protection, health
Marigold	Protection, boosts intuition
Mint	Love, increasing sexual desire, healing, banishing
Mugwort	Female sexual organ tonic, healing
Oak	Knowledge, power and independence, confidence, potency

Name	Wisdom
Olive	Peace, companionship, forgiveness
Orange	Love, happiness
Passionflower	Endurance, friendship
Pennyroyal	Female stimulant
Pine	Purification
Raspberry Leaf	Strength, uterine tonic, promotes flexibility
Rose	Aphrodisiac, beauty, connection, long-lasting love
Rosemary	Love, passion, strategy, banishes negativity and depression
Rue	Female lust
Sage	Wisdom, protection, purification
Saffron	Lust, fertility, 'higher love'
Sandalwood	Protection, healing, relaxing, attraction
Sarsaparilla	Love, attraction
Snake Root	Abundance
Snapdragon	Keeping secrets, recovery, reclaiming
Southern Wood	Masculine energy, love, lust
Squaw Vine	Feminine balance, hormonal healer, solidness
St John's Wort	Health, love divination, happiness
Sunflower	Developing potential, confidence, self-esteem
Tansy	Health, longevity, new starts
Tiger Lily	Purity, wildness
Valerian	Peace, relaxation, love divination, banishes despair
Vervain	Lust, seduction
Violet	Purification, modesty, uncovering
Walnut	Intelligence, strategy
Willow	Feminine divine, flexibility, truth
Witch Hazel	Mends broken hearts, clarifying
Witchbane	Transformational, attracts good energy, banishes negative
Witches Grass	Attraction, releases intensity
Yarrow	Promotes long term love, courage

Bathing

There really is nothing as relaxing as a long hot bath! Add some delectable herbs, flowers and plant oils and you have a superbly restful place to be – and a magical one too!

Allow us to suggest a mixture of a few drops of jasmine oil, a stick or two of cinnamon bark, a handful of rose petals and a pinch of fresh basil leaves for a romantic yet sensual bath that both stimulates and relaxes at the same time. This one is perfect before that hot date or big night out.

Anointing

Using the essential oils to mark or 'anoint' an object charges it with the energies inherent in the oils itself. In ancient times, warriors would rub a blend of oils and herbs into their blades before battle to ensure flow, luck and divine guidance in battle. Many spiritual practitioners today anoint their magical tools or create talismans (charged objects) to dedicate them towards a certain purpose. You can have the same benefits by anointing a piece of jewellery to wear when you go out for 'attraction' or even a small crystal to place in your pocket to purify things after a nasty break-up.

Essential Oils

Aromatherapy is a type of alternative medicine which uses the specific aromas from essential oils to help heal many different medical conditions. The essential oils can also be used to attract energy and to clear or enhance an area or environment around a person.

100% pure essential oils are the best to use. They can be mixed with base carrier oils such as evening primrose oil, avocado oil or sesame oil and be burnt in oil burners or placed on the wrists or neck as a perfume.

Sprays or spritzers with essential oils and flower essences can be sprayed in and around a room or over your body. Jade has her own personal line of sprays and perfumes available to help clear negativity and attract positivity and love into your life.

Essential oils can be purchased from many chemists, health food stores, naturopath clinics or new age shops.

Do take care, though, with essential oils and the respective dosages ... usually a few drops each in a tablespoon of carrier oil is enough and always check the contra-indications especially if you are pregnant or taking medication. Do not apply undiluted essential oils onto the skin. A skin patch test should be conducted prior to using oil that you've never used before.

Never ingest essential oils.

Give children only the gentlest oils, such as mandarin, at extremely low doses. It is safest to consult a qualified aromatherapy practitioner before using oils with children.

We recommend the use of the following essential oils to help you with your relationship area:

Essential Oils

Oil	Symbol	Energy to attract
Rose	Love	Opens the Heart
		Reproductive Organs
Orange or Mandarin	Refreshing	Detoxifying
		Positivity
Frankincense	Relaxing	Uplifting
		Anti Depressant
Bergamot	Uplifting	Refreshing
		Energising
Ylang Ylang	Stimulating	Helps sexual dysfunction
		Aphrodisiac
Jasmine	Soothing	Confidence
		Relaxing
Patchouli	Calming	Increase Libido
		Happiness
Ginger	Warming	Adds energy and spice
		Stimulation
Juniper Berry	Cleansing	Refreshing
		Uplifting

Feng Shui

Feng Shui is the ancient Chinese technique of placing objects around your home or work environments in specific areas to harmonise the chi (energy). By using Feng Shui in your home or bedroom you can increase your chances of attracting a great relationship or enhance an existing relationship and achieve a positive energy flow in and around you.

Feng Shui is a very in-depth topic, so for our purposes we will be focusing on a few quick tips for your relationship area and bedroom.

Tips to get your relationship area moving:

- clear the clutter out of your bedroom, remove any excess furniture or clothes, make room for new relationship energy
- remove stale energy with space clearing sprays, essential oil burners, scented candles or incense
- clear out any gym or sporting equipment from the bedroom; this is to keep your bedroom relaxed and not focused on hard work
- place your bed against a solid wall, don't have your feet facing out the door when you are lying in bed (in the coffin position)
- have a bed with a large sturdy bedhead for strong foundations
- use warm, sensual colours on the furnishings and bed linen, e.g. deep purples, reds, burgundies, oranges, golds, browns
- remove the ex, get rid of anything that reminds you of the ex partner
- try to have items in pairs such as two statues, photos with two people, two candles together as this encourages equality and a sense of we – not me – in a relationship
- place rose quartz and coloured candles in your bedroom
- bring romantic items into your bedroom such as beautiful sensual artwork, big velvet blankets and soft silky pillows.

Vision Boards

A vision board is a focal point that sends your wishes and dreams out to the Universe. It may sound a bit airy-fairy but it is actually very powerful and has produced great results for many people.

Your vision board should be your visual wish list. It is a way for you to stay focused on your goals, to have a visual reminder and to also keep you motivated on what you want to achieve.

It's important that you take some time to sit quietly before you start making your vision board. Take time to think about what it is that you would like to attract into your life and your relationship area. Set your intent; be clear about what it is you would like to attract.

CREATING A VISION BOARD

When you are ready to make your vision board you will need a few different materials. They are as follows:

- Glue or sticky tape
- A large piece of paper or cardboard, or a large cork or whiteboard
- Scissors
- Pens, pencils or crayons
- Coloured paper (if you like)
- Old newspapers, photos, magazines, shop catalogues

It is very easy to make your vision board; it is meant to be relaxing, creative and fun. There are no set, hard and fast rules that you need to stick to. Your vision board does not need to be a balanced, amazing piece of artwork; it is only for you to see – so have fun with it.

1. Grab your piece of cardboard, paper or board.
2. Go through your newspapers, magazines, photos and shop catalogues and tear or cut out any images or words that may stand out to you.

Anything that makes you feel excited or something that you would like to have in your life.

For example a picture of a happy couple hugging and smiling or the word 'LOVE', 'Health' or 'Happiness'.

If you want children, perhaps a photo with a couple and their kids smiling.

If there are no pictures or words that you can find, write them down yourself on a piece of coloured paper.

3. You may want to stick your action plan on your vision board, or the list of your deal breakers and negotiables.

4. You may wish to have a photo or picture of yourself on the vision board; just make sure it's a positive photo that makes you feel good when you look at it.

5. When you are ready glue or stick all of the images, words or photos onto your vision board. You will intuitively know where you should stick everything.

6. It's important to place your vision board in a place that you can see it on a regular basis (you may want to put it in your bedroom as it is a private thing).

7. Try to update your vision board whenever you feel you need to. You don't need to just make your vision board once, it's important to chop and change things as you need to.

There are not only physical tools such as those that we have listed above – herbs, candles, crystals etc – there are also some very powerful Goddesses and Gods which can be called upon to help you to improve your life and in particular your relationship area.

The many faces of the Divine: Goddesses and Gods

The Divine takes many faces and forms across time and culture. Just as each of us on this earth is unique, it seems there is a god and/

or goddess that fits everyone's ideal. Similarly, as we all have complex personalities and resonate to different paths, so too do the Gods and Goddesses.

The Divine has always appeared in a form that we can relate and connect with. An Egyptian God looks Egyptian. An African Goddess is dark-skinned and beaded. For warriors, She is a Warrior. For those seeking Beauty, She is Beautiful. Each form, each face, developed a 'specialty energy' that we could relate and aspire to.

Many spiritual paths, including that of the Witch, believe that the Goddess/God lives in us and so we too carry the spark of the divine. This enables us to choose from those different faces to assist us with our imbalance or incompleteness.

We can choose to ask a God whose 'specialty energy' is removing obstacles to obstacle-bust that stubborn belief that is in our way to greatness! We can choose a Goddess whose mythology tells us she is wonderful at birthing new beginnings and ask her for help when we are struggling with that raw time after a break up. Stacey will often call upon the specific wisdom that the Goddess Brigid has when writing as she offers great creative flow through the arts.

Every day we see the empowerment that results in calling upon these many faces of the Divine to back us up and to make things easier when it comes to relationships. One of our clients calls upon the Japanese Goddess Amaterasu when she feels she is having a 'bad body day' to help her feel better about her body image. Commonly, many men call upon Osiris when they wish to conceive a child or many women call upon the stunning Nordic Queen, Freya, for assistance with raising sexual sizzle!

You may have never thought about asking for help from a God or Goddess or you may find you have already discovered the advantages of doing so. You can 'invoke' these energies in a variety of ways.

The simplest way is to light a candle, breathe deeply, ask for what you need and ask for them to be present and to help you. Use your own words; you need not come up with anything too fancy if you are not that way inclined. If you have more time, you may wish to add something associated with that Deity to the spot next to the candle, as this further honours them.

For example, Artemis loves dogs and forests, so adding a few hairs from your dog (don't pull them out as we are sure there would be a few on the floor somewhere!) or a few forest leaves as a welcome for her.

Freya loves amber, Dionysis loves wine and Poseidon, of course, loves all things from the sea. You can have fun with this as well as gaining the benefits!

Below we have compiled a table of Gods and Goddesses whose energies may be useful to you in the sphere of Soul Mates and soul monsters.

God Table

God	Wisdom
Apollo	Wisdom, leadership, divorce/custody inquiry
Ares/Mars	Confrontation, fertility, strategy
Balarama	Strength, fertility
Coyote	Transformation, growth, transition, to take oneself lightly
Cronus/Saturn	Patience, using size to one's advantage, sexual fertility
Dionysus	Play, wine, decadence, pleasure, sexual abandonment, ecstasy
Hades/Hephaistos	Death of old, shadow side, releasing old habits
Hermes/Mercury	Technology, speed in communicating, clarity
Krishna	Love, goodness, leadership, equality
Lao Tzu	Passion, lust
Loki	Play/tricking, emotional blackmail/dishonesty, lightening up
Osiris	Wholeness, rebirth/birth, sperm quality, committed love, masculine fertility

God	Wisdom
Poseidon/Neptune	Making waves, breaking through obstacles, healthy fierceness, anger
Ptah	Creativity, skills, leadership
Raven	Communication, calm debating, intuition
Thoth	Wisdom, wholeness, magic, health, journalling, learning
Thor	Freedom, creativity, healthy fierceness, physical action, rut-buster!
Thunderbird	Beginnings, fertility, ideas, creativity
Vishnu	Protection, faith without doubt, deep love
Zeus/Jupiter, Jove	Co-dependence buster, game playing/strategy, equality, strength

Goddess Table

Goddess	Wisdom
Amaterasu	Appreciation of our own beauty, confidence
Aphrodite/Venus	Self-love, romantic love, beauty, desire, passion
Artemis/Diana	Independence, connection on your own terms, courage, self-trust, co-dependence and addiction buster
Astarte	Guidance, correct decision making for you and family
Athena/Minerva	Wisdom, good counsel, justice, decisiveness
Baba Yaga	Allowing wildness, independence, personal freedom and joy, storytelling
Bast	Pleasure, laughter, joy, play, depression buster
Brigit/Brigid	Creativity, fertility, ideas, easy conception
Ceres/Demeter	Knowing the harvest of your life, growth, participation, plenty
Cerridwen	Cycle of birth/death/rebirth, protection, tolerance, acceptance, integration
Eostre	Helps hormonal imbalances, new beginnings, fertility, conception
Eurynome	Sexual abandonment, ecstasy, connection through sex or pleasure
Freya	Love of self and body, joy in our own sexual power, birth, fertility, attraction
Gaia/Tellus	Mother Earth, abundance, creativity, growth, cycles
Hathor	Contentment, quiet joy, unconditional love

Hecate/Trivia	Births/deaths, beginnings/endings, cutting cords
Hera	Protective, power with confidence, tradition
Hestia/Vesta	Making the home a sanctuary, protection
Inanna	Embracing your shadow side, honestly discovering one's faults, honour, The Mother
Ishtar	Goddess of war, strategy, healthy fierceness, victory
Isis	The Mother, birth, care of others, strategy, committed love
Ixchel	Healing through creativity, resilience, purpose
Kali	The destroyer as a catalyst for change, the healthy expression of emotions
Kwan Yin	Compassion for self and others
Lakshmi	Abundance
Lillith	Female independence, power being taken back, equality
Maat	Justice, fair order
Mary	Unconditional love, mercy and compassion under difficult conditions
Morgan le Faye	Dancing to your own drum, authenticity
Oshun	Sensuality, power through the senses
Oya	Welcoming change, change management, protective
Pachamama	Healing and becoming whole, completion
Pele	Healthy expression of emotions, fire and passion
Persephone/Kore	Planning for growth, death of one thing to makespace for the new
Rhiannon	Fighting doubt, speaking up, fear
Sarawati	Listening, learning, breakthroughs
Sekhmet	Cord cutting, expression of healthy anger rather than rage, boundaries
Shakti	Sexual energy, surrender, connection
Spider Woman	Connection with the wider world, wisdom, patience, strategy
Tara	Compassion, protection, acceptance, liberation
Yemaya	Surrender/Faith, strength in risk taking

CONCLUSION

SOME FINAL NO EXCUSES ...

If there is one thing you take out of this book, it's that you don't need to be held back in your life by your relationships.

By being forearmed, by being able to identify what kind of Soul Mates enter your life and knowing what soul monsters may lurk in your way, things should be far less painful. You have also learnt how to trap those soul monsters and kill them off by Cutting the Cords — so you can blast through any obstacle that is holding you back.

It is up to you now to take your own power into your hands. Do not be tempted to fall back and settle into old belief systems or habits. Move forward with no excuses!

If you do feel yourself slipping backwards, that's understandable, we are all works in progress ... that's the cool bit! Consciously stop yourself and begin to focus on the positives in your life once more and things will begin to swing your way again.

You have read about the many different tools and ways to move forward in your life and relationships. Try these with curiosity and see what brings you the greatest benefit.

Most importantly, you now know that by living a great life you will begin to generate a tsunami of great energy that attracts the kind of relationship you want. By participating in all of the things you love to do and by living your life in a connected, positive way, you cannot help to attract a likeminded partner. Like attracts like even in scientific circles! It's a win–win situation, because you are living the life you want and you are also able to share the journey with someone else.

Know that you can have a complete, happy and fulfilling life without having an intimate relationship/partner, but paradoxically, by doing this, you are more likely to attract one.

We would love to hear from you about your experiences in moving forward with our 'No Excuses' techniques. We would love to have the honour of working with you during a workshop or consult. One of our greatest joys is getting that wedding invitation in the mail or as we did just today an email headed 'I've found her!'

Live, love and laugh!

With No Excuses …

Stacey and Jade

XXX

Appendix

Resources

Private Consultations or Readings

Should you wish to contact or book an Oracle Consultation, Cutting the Cords or Personal Spellcasting with Stacey Demarco please visit:

www.themodernwitch.com

or to contact or book a Psychic, Mediumship or Past Life reading with Jade-Sky please visit:

www.jade-sky.com.au

Additionally, our sites are a resource-rich place for information and products that will assist you further.

Feng Shui

For a holistic approach we recommend Thomas Walsh: wuweidragon@gmail.com

Association of Feng Shui Consultants: www.afsc.org.au

Workshops, Lecture Programs and Books for Stacey and Jade

RCM Management: www.rcmmanagement.com

With No Excuses Workshops: www.withnoexcuses.com.au

Meditation and Audio Programs

Including:

Cutting the Cords: www.themodernwitch.com

Spell to Attract your Ideal Partner: www.themodernwitch.com

Meditations to Determine Past Lives: www.jade-sky.com.au

Meditations to meet your Animal Guides: www.jade-sky.com.au

Talismans

Beautiful and powerful Goddess and Animal Talismans, blessed and charged through ritual, are available in limited numbers through www.themodernwitch.com

Herbs

Spell-ready herbs available through www.themodernwitch.com

Crystals

For rare and hard to get crystals contact Brett Laing: blaing26@optusnet.com.au or through www.facebook.com/brettlaing

Soy Candles and Space Clearing Sprays with Essential Oils

100% Natural Soy Candles with essential oils and a crystal for abundance, protection, love or guidance available through: www.jade-sky.com.au
Essential oil and flower essence, space clearing sprays for abundance, protection, love or guidance available through: www.jade-sky.com.au

Other

Australian Psychics Association:

www.newagesupastore.com/apa/membership.php

The Pagan Awareness Network www.paganawareness.net.au

ABOUT THE AUTHORS

STACEY DEMARCO

Stacey Demarco, once described as *The thinking woman's Witch*, was the metaphysical expert on the hit Australian TV series, *The One*. She is the author of three successful books: *Witch in the Boardroom, Witch in the Bedroom* and *The Coffee Oracle*.

She is a committee member of the Pagan Awareness Network and a life member of the Australian Psychics Association.

Stacey is an ardent traveller, horsewoman and photographer. She lives by the sea in the beautiful Northern Beaches of Sydney, Australia with her husband and her animal companions.

Visit: www.themodernwitch.com

JADE-SKY

Mediumship is Jade-Sky's passion. During a reading she offers up key names, dates and specific events to the enquirer so that they know, without doubt, that their passed loved ones or spirit guides/angels are with them. She also provides very personal and significant details to help clients reconnect with their loved ones, something which assists with their grieving process.

By giving detailed information, Jade-Sky reassures her clients that life after death does exist and a beautiful place awaits us when we pass from this life to the next.

As well as conducting private readings and workshops, Jade-Sky has spoken and appeared live on stage at Mind, Body, Spirit Festivals and national print and radio stations around Australia..

Based in Brisbane, Australia; Jade-Sky travels extensively and can do so on several planes, be them spiritual or physical!

Visit : www.jade-sky.com.au